THE SECRETS OF
PHOENIX-EYE FIST KUNG-FU

The Art of Chuka Shaolin

Cheong Cheng Leong

&

Mark V. Wiley

TUTTLE PUBLISHING

BOSTON • RUTLAND, VERMONT • TOKYO

This edition published in 2000 by Tuttle Publishing, an imprint of Periplus Editions (HK) Ltd., with editorial offices at 153 Milk Street, Boston, Massachusetts, 02109.

Library of Congress Cataloging-in-Publication Data

Cheong, Cheng Leong, 1940-
    The secrets of phoenix-eye fist Kung fu : the art of chuka shaolin / Cheong Cheng Leong & Mark V. Wiley.-- 1st ed.
        p.cm.
    ISBN 0-8048-3178-5 (pbk.)
        1. Kung fu. I. Wiley, Mark V. II. Title.

GV1114.7 .C43 2000
796.815'5--dc21

00-041178

Distributed by

North America
Tuttle Publishing
Distribution Center
Airport Industrial Park
364 Innovation Drive
North Clarendon, VT 05759-9436
Tel: (802) 773-8930
Tel: (800) 526-2778
Fax: (802) 773-6993

Japan
Tuttle Publishing
RK Building, 2nd Floor
2-13-10 Shimo-Meguro, Meguro-Ku
Tokyo 153 0064
Tel: (03) 5437-0171
Tel: (03) 5437-0755

Asia Pacific
Berkeley Books Pte Ltd
5 Little Road #08-01
Singapore 536983
Tel: (65) 280-1330
Fax: (65) 280-6290

05 04 03 02 01 00   9 8 7 6 5 4 3 2 1

Printed in the United States of America

For the Cheong family and Master Lee Siong Pheow

Wu-Shu Zhao Zhuen

Hong Yang Gao Chue

"To unite and gain superiority for our martial arts"

"To promote and propagate our national purity"

[Calligraphy written by Pai Shen, the late abbot of Penang's Kek Lok Si Temple, when he was eighty years old. It was presented to Grandmaster Cheong Cheng Leong as a gift and memento of his selfless, lifelong promotion of Chinese martial art and culture.]

CONTENTS

PART ONE: CHUKA SHAOLIN IN PERSPECTIVE

PART TWO: THE EMPTY-HAND ART

PART FOUR: THE HEALING ART

I was first introduced to the rare art of phoenix-eye fist kung-fu in 1986 through a book co-written by the art's headmaster, Cheong Cheng Leong, and the late hoplologist, Donn F. Draeger. At the time, I was working for Asian World of Martial Arts, one of the largest suppliers and stores of martial arts books and equipment in the world. One evening after work, my co-worker Carlos Aldrete-Phan and I were relaxing in his apartment talking about all the different kinds of martial arts there were in the world. Being well-read and having practiced a number of different systems, I was rattling off a shopping list of names and countries of origin. Carlos stopped me midstream and asked if I had ever heard of the art of Chuka Shaolin. I replied that I hadn't. Carlos then asked if I had ever heard of a writer named Donn Draeger. I replied that of course I had, as he was quite famous. Carlos then pulled a book off his shelf titled *Phoenix-Eye Fist: A Shaolin Fighting Art of South China,* by Cheong Cheng Leong and Donn F. Draeger. He handed it to me.

After browsing through the first couple of pages I found that the proper name of the phoenix-eye fist art was Chuka Shaolin, and that it was an offshoot of Fukien Shaolin boxing. What struck me most about the art was its primary use of the phoenix-eye fist hand formation for striking—hence its more popular name. After a few minutes I looked up from the book to see a big smile across Carlos' face. We were both thinking the same thing: One day we would train in and master the art of the phoenix-eye fist. The only problem was that the master of the art, Cheong Cheng Leong, resided in Malaysia, and there were no instructors of the art in the United States. Well, at least we had the book.

While I never attempted to learn the art from the book, it did give me a sense of the use of the phoenix-eye fist hand formation and of the theory behind its use. Carlos, on the other hand, endeavored to memorize the solo empty-hand form it presented.

It wasn't until 1996—a full ten years later—that I was able to travel from the Philippines to Malaysia to meet Cheong Cheng Leong in person. And what a meeting it was. Several months prior to the trip, I was given the necessary contact information for Mr. Cheong by Hunter Armstrong, director of the International Hoplology Society. Chip, as Hunter is known to his friends, directed me to a man named Karunakaran, who had been Draeger's top student and who continues to run Draeger's jo-jutsu dojo in Malaysia. Upon my arrival in Penang, Mr. Karuna (as I call him) took me to meet Mr. Leong at his *kwoon* on the steps leading up to the Kek Lok Si Temple in the Air Itam area of Penang.

I was given a full-blown demonstration of Chuka Shaolin, including several empty-hand forms, a few two-person forms, several demonstrations of weapons forms, as well as training drills and technique applications. Wow! There was so much to be found in this art. I had no idea. From reading the book, I had assumed that the art was merely an empty-hand system. How wrong I was. At that moment I knew what had to be done: another book must be written!

Before I was given a chance to present Mr. Leong with my idea for a book, I first had to give a demonstration of my own. So, I stepped onto the floor and demonstrated three empty-hand forms from the *ngo cho kun* style of kung-fu. I chose to demonstrate this art because it hails from the same area in China as Chuka Shaolin. I thought that any link, even a tenuous one, would make Mr. Leong more amenable to allowing me, a stranger, to co-write a book with him.

After my demonstration I sat down and interviewed Mr. Leong for a possible magazine article to go with the photographs I had taken during his demonstration. Since he did not know me very well, I was a bit reluctant to ask him if I could co-write a book with him, as Draeger had done nineteen years earlier. So I took a minute to gather my thoughts and formulate my argument for the need of such a book. (More than anything, though, my need was to pick his brain and learn the inner workings of his art!) In any event, since his book with Draeger had been out of print for some ten years at that point, I figured I had nothing to lose, so I asked.

Mr. Leong immediately agreed. In fact, he was enthusiastic about the idea. We decided that we would present the information in the first book again, but in an abbreviated fashion, and then present a second empty-hand form, followed by a weapon form and its applications.

Between 1996 and 1999, I made three trips to Malaysia to work with Cheong Cheng Leong on the book you now hold in your hands. During this time, however, the first book came back into print, which was both good and bad news. Since the first book was published by Weatherhill and this new book was to be published by Tuttle, it would be a conflict of interest (and perhaps a legal problem) to present the same information. So, after some discussion, Mr. Leong and I decided to present in the new book a more detailed history of the art, historical photographs that did not appear in the first book, a two-person empty-hand fighting form (so that those interested in learning how to train and apply the empty-hand form presented in the first book would have a means of doing so), the basics necessary to correctly execute the two-person empty-hand fighting form, one of the two pole forms, an overview of all the Chuka weapons, a few applications of each, two-person strength and conditioning exercises, and the chi kung and healing dimensions of the art, which had not been written about before.

This was the rationale behind the presentation of information in this book and how Mr. Leong and I came together to write it. And while both of the books on Chuka Shaolin are good in and of themselves, as a set they are indispensable. The information presented in the two books, when combined, truly gives those interested in learning the art of the phoenix-eye fist a complete overview of the art and the ins and outs of training.

It is truly my honor to have made the acquaintance of Mr. Leong and to have been given the opportunity to write a book with him. While all of the technical information is from Cheong Cheng Leong's vast knowledge of the art, the actual writing of the book was done by me. I must state, therefore, that if there are any faults with this volume in terms of presentation of material, they are my own. And if they are major, I offer my apologies to Grandmaster Cheong Cheng Leong and to those aspiring to learn this rare and dynamic fighting art.

—*Mark V. Wiley*
Towson, MD

INTRODUCTION

Over the past fifty years martial arts have seen a rise in popularity never seen at any other time. Along with this popularity, though, has come a watering down of the traditional kung-fu methods. That is to say, the original purpose of the arts as systems of self-defense and physical and mental disciplines has turned into aerobic and gymnastic performance activities.

Due to the recent changes in the People's Republic of China, martial arts there have taken on a unique flavor, one based on the utilitarian role they are seen as fulfilling. With the aesthetic aspects of the art being stressed, and as a result of the persecution of martial artists during the ten years of the Cultural Revolution (1966–1976), the practical aspects are often downplayed, and it is arguable that the overall level of skill in the combative elements of the arts has greatly declined.

The purpose of this book, then, is to not only preserve one of the most dynamic and realistic Chinese fighting arts in existence, but to provide the reader with a broader view of the art of Chuka Shaolin than has previously been available.

This current work is divided into four parts, each focusing on a different dimension of the art. Part One, "Chuka Shaolin in Perspective," sets the tone for the book by presenting a detailed history of the art from its parent art of Fukien Shaolin to its formation at the hands of the Chu sisters, through several generations of masters, up until the present time. This section also offers an overview in terms of how a student learns the art and the fighting principles that enable the practitioner to effectively apply the art when necessary.

Part Two, "The Empty-Hand Art," gives an overview of the basic stances, hand techniques, and foot techniques used in the art in general—yet also specific to the two-person fighting form presented later in the book—as well as descriptions and photographs of the empty-hand two-person form. By practicing this form, exponents learn the proper distances, angles, and psychological mind-set necessary when attempting to apply the empty-hand techniques against an opponent. This section also presents five strength and conditioning exercises, diligent practice of which will better enable the Chuka practitioner to execute his techniques, absorb the impact of his opponent's techniques, as well as develop his own gripping, pulling, and pushing power without the use of external training devices.

Part Three, "The Weapon Art," offers an overview of the weapons used in Chuka Shaolin, which includes the pole, long spear, iron rulers, twin knives, and farmer's hoe. The six-and-a-half-point pole form is then presented, along with fighting applications of the pole and other weapons.

Part Four, "The Healing Art," discusses the little-known healing dimensions of Chuka Shaolin. This section provides a discussion on the use and practice of chi kung, or internal energy exercises, and presents an overview of the impact healing art used to treat old injuries to the musculoskeletal system.

The book concludes with an afterword, a lineage of the art's masters and teachers, and a complete list of the solo and two-person empty-hand and weapon forms found within the system. In the interest of keeping the text easy to read, most of the art's terms are presented in English. For those interested in the original Chinese spellings, a glossary of terms in English and Mandarin is found at the end of the book.

We hope this book has something to offer all martial artists, beginners and advanced, Chuka stylists and exponents of other arts alike. It should be noted that this book was not written in a vacuum, but represents, instead, the efforts of many individuals. We would, therefore, like to thank the following for their respective contributions to this project: Tan Hun Poey, Cheong Boo Kheng, Ong Tatt Lin, Woo Kim Hin, the Lam family, Ron Beaubien, Karunakaran A/L R. Chindan, Hunter B. Armstrong, Carlos Aldrete-Phan, Robert Chu, Alex Co., and the late Donn F. Draeger.

—Cheong Cheng Leong
& Mark V. Wiley,
Penang, 1999

CHAPTER ONE

Historical Perspective

The historical documentation of a fighting art that spans several hundred years is a difficult undertaking. This is especially so when the art in question lacks written documentation prior to the 1970s, as is the case with Chuka Shaolin. And while Cheong Cheng Leong knows the history of his art as passed on to him by his late master, Lee Siong Pheow, he is unsure of the origins of the art past five generations.

In an attempt to be as accurate and as detailed as possible, we not only present the oral history of Chuka Shaolin as passed down through the generations, but we also offer several new insights into the "mother art(s)" from which it may have sprung.

One possible origin of Chuka Shaolin is found among the Hakka, or Guest Family, peoples of Canton/Guangdong, China. There is a martial art among the Hakka people that stems from *Chu gar kow,* or the Chu family religion. *Chu gar kow* was originally an underground society that formed during the Qing/Manchu dynasties. *Chu gar kow's* fighting art is now known to many as *Chu-gar* mantis, the first of the "southern" praying mantis systems to have developed. Over the years, other styles of southern mantis, such as *Chow-gar* and *jook lum* have also evolved. Since the Chinese characters for *Chu-gar* (southern praying mantis) and *Chuka* (phoenix-eye fist) are the same, it is possible that the latter art evolved from the former.

Another possible origin of Chuka Shaolin is Fukien white crane boxing. Some believe that the teachings of the *Chu gar kow* spread and became the various styles of Fukien Shaolin boxing—of which white crane boxing is a part. Since the cave where the nun Leow Fah Shih Koo resided and later taught her "Shaolin" art to the Chu sisters was known as the *Pai-Ho Toong,* or White Crane Cave, it is possible that Chuka Shaolin is based in *pai-ho,* or southern white crane, kung-fu.

Perhaps a more feasible explanation is that the art evolved as an eclectic blend of several Fukien Shaolin arts, including white crane boxing and *Chu-gar* praying mantis boxing.

However, like so many other martial arts, the history of Chuka Shaolin is shrouded in the myths and legends of oral traditions passed down through the generations from master to disciple. In the case of the art in question, oral history holds that it was founded by a Shaolin nun who, after leaving the Shaolin Temple, passed on her art to two sisters with the surname Chu.

The story goes something like this . . .

A Nun and Two Sisters

In the late eighteenth century, there was a Buddhist nun named Leow Fah Shih Koo who was said to have attained mastery of Shaolin kung-fu at

China's Fukien Shaolin Temple. She learned the art from her brother, Abbot Chih Sun. During a time of political turmoil, Leow left Shaolin to seek a more peaceful and quite life for herself in the *Pai-Ho Toong,* or White Crane Cave, in Kwangtung province.

Aside from her skills in Shaolin kung-fu, Leow was also an herbalist. In fact, she earned her living by gathering and compounding herbs from the hillsides and selling them in a nearby town.

One day, while en route to town to sell her herbs, Leow chanced upon two sisters who had been abandoned and left to fend for themselves in the village granary. Upon further investigation, Leow found that the sisters were Chu Meow Eng and Chu Meow Luan, daughters of wealthy parents who had recently been robbed and murdered.

Leow took the children into her cave-home and raised them as her own. The Chu sisters assisted the nun in the collection of herbs and the preparation of compounds for sale in the village. In addition, Leow taught them Shaolin kung-fu, an art at which they excelled. In fact, it is said that the Chu sisters were so talented that they were able to master the Shaolin art after just a few years of dedicated practice. It was upon their completion of Shaolin training that Leow encouraged them to study the fighting instincts and techniques of animals and insects. With this in mind, the Chu sisters then embarked on observing and imitating the fighting actions of the praying mantis, tiger, monkey, and snake. They then incorporated these new skills into the Shaolin art taught to them by Leow. Elements of the praying mantis, tiger, monkey, and snake can be found in varying degrees in the empty-hand forms of this dynamic fighting art.

After perfecting their new fighting art, the Chu sisters presented it to the nun for review and criticism. Leow was so impressed that she formally named the new art "Chuka" from *Chu,* the sisters' surname, and *ka,* meaning "family" in the Hakka dialect. Thus, Chuka refers to the Chu-family style of Chinese martial arts. And while not a Shaolin martial art proper, and actually having developed independent of the temple itself, in deference to the Fukien Shaolin Temple wherein Leow learned her fighting art, the name was carried over. Thus, the complete name of the Chu sisters' art became Chuka Shaolin.

It was also during this time that the nun envisioned and came to develop the deadly hand-formation resembling the eye of the mythical phoenix. Feeling that this particular fist strike was especially effective for women (i.e., herself and the Chu sisters), Leow incorporated it into the Chu sisters' new fighting art. As time passed, however, the exponents of Chuka Shaolin began to favor the use of the phoenix-eye fist hand strike. As a result, the art of Chuka Shaolin is now more commonly known as phoenix-eye fist kung-fu.

OOH PING KWANG

After Leow passed away, the Chu sisters embraced her kind disposition and continued to gather herbs, make medicinal compounds, and practice kung-fu. One day while on their way to town, one of the sisters was accidentally struck by mud thrown by a group of boys who were fighting. Upon seeing that a passerby had been struck with the mud, all the boys fled, with the exception of the one who had actually flung the mud. The boy apologized profusely for the accident, stating that he was merely flinging mud in all directions so as to keep the bullies from getting at him.

The boy's name was Ooh Ping Kwang. He was an orphan who tended the cows and did other chores on his uncle's farm in exchange for his keep. The sisters were so impressed with the boy's disposition and honesty that they approached Ooh's uncle and asked permission to look after the boy.

The sympathetic uncle said he would consent only if the sisters agreed to teach his nephew their martial art in an effort to secure a safer future for the frail child. The nuns agreed. Ooh was nine years old at the time.

Over the many years Ooh served the Chu sisters he grew to manhood and became quite skilled as a martial artist and as an herbalist. On the death of the second Chu sister, Ooh, now almost forty, descended from his cave-home and settled in the village, where he married a local girl. Ooh then set about imparting the Chuka art and herbal knowledge to his relatives and trusted friends, never forgetting the Chu sisters, their strict teachings, and their high moral character.

LEE SIONG PHEOW

Lee Siong Pheow (1886–1961) was one of Ooh's most gifted disciples. He was trained in a more rigorous manner than any of Ooh's other pupils, serving a long apprenticeship with the master. Lee worked hard during the day, fully occupied with the domestic chores in his master's household. Every evening and early each morning Ooh directed Lee's Chuka training. Lee was required to undergo unremitting practice of the various stances and postures, an unnerving and boring practice to be sure, but he persevered. Lee's only problem was his temper. While he willingly accepted the hard work and the beatings administered by his master, and whatever harsh punishment the master might decree to correct any mistakes made in training, Lee could not accept domination by others.

One day, Lee's temper got the better of him. He relentlessly beat Master Ooh's son during training. For this unforgivable act, Master Ooh, using a long hardwood pole, fiercely struck Lee's fist and foot, crippling the index finger of his right hand and deforming one of his feet for life. While such a severe lesson would surely have discouraged a spiritually weaker man, it only served to make Lee realize that his skill was not yet perfect. He had to train even harder than in the past. In time, Lee's diligent effort and consistent training elevated him to the highest level of Chuka Shaolin excellence, and it is said that no local fighter could defeat him in one-on-one combat.

In 1930, Lee left Kwangtung and emigrated to Malaysia, where he settled in Penang and earned his living as an herbalist and traditional physician (fig. 1). He followed the strict traditional policies of his Chuka predecessors, especially the rule of choosing students with wisdom and great care. Lee required that each candidate who wished to study under him accept certain conditions. The candidate was to kneel before him holding a cup of Chinese tea in one hand and a small red envelope containing money in the other. By this method, Lee tested the candidate's humility and sincerity. Many refused to kneel before the master, instead issuing pompous challenges of fighting skill. Lee, a man said to have never refused a challenge, obliged. As in China, Lee was never known to have been defeated in Malaysia. Many, after being defeated and thoroughly embarrassed at the hands of Master Lee, had an immediate change of heart and, in the manner Lee required, asked to be accepted as a student. Once accepted as a pupil, Lee inculcated them with three principles:

- Do not create or seek trouble.

- Do not teach people of unproved character what you have learned.

- Always be humble and respectful to others.

Indeed, a breach of any of these principles meant instant expulsion from the art. Master Lee was said to have never given an offender a second chance.

Master Lee passed away in 1961, at the age of seventy-seven. His most prized pupil was Cheong Cheng Leong, the current grandmaster of the art.

Fig. 1

Lee Siong Pheow

CHEONG CHENG LEONG

Cheong Cheng Leong began his study of Chuka Shaolin under the tutelage of Master Lee Siong Pheow in 1951, at the impressionable age of ten (eleven, by the Chinese calendar). Master Lee, who was already in his sixties at this time, was famous in the Air Itam quarter of Pulau Pinang, Malaysia. Someone had told Cheong that there was a master in the town who knew a very special type of fist that was strong and could surely kill anybody, regardless of size and fighting ability. Being a young and impressionable boy who liked to fight, Cheong approached the master, determined to learn his art (fig. 2). At that time, Lee taught only Chinese of Cantonese or Hakka status, no Hokkien. Fortunately for the future of the art, Cheong Cheng Leong was a member of the correct social class.

Fig. 2

Cheong Cheng Leong

Master Lee was interested in Cheong and his friends because they were so young and impressionable; he believed that he could mold them into respectable and upstanding citizens. When he approached Lee, the master asked Cheong if he was interested in learning Chuka Shaolin to become a better fighter. Cheong answered no, he was not interested in the art for fighting. Master Lee then asked the young Cheong why, if not for fighting, he wished to learn kung-fu. Cheong sat there in silence. Master Lee again asked Cheong if he was sincerely not interested in the art for purposes of fighting. Cheong replied that he was really not interested in such things. With that, Master Lee seemed content and said since Cheong was not interested in fighting, he would accept the boy as a student.

Master Lee still adhered to the ceremony of accepting new pupils, but Cheong was young and forgot all that was expected of him in this regard. He simply stuffed five Malaysian dollars into a red envelope and handed it to the master. At that time, five Malaysian dollars was quite expensive for kung-fu training in Malaysia. After all, one could join any of the other martial arts associations in Penang, like Chin Wu, for only one or two dollars. However, money seemed no object for some, and a few people who could afford it paid Master Lee fifty Malaysian dollars for lessons! These people thought that with the extra money changing hands, they were afforded special attention and training by the master. Cheong, however, is of the opinion that they learned nothing special as a result.

Cheong and his friends used to hang out and fight on the banks of the Air Itam river—nice water, nice fishing, nice fighting. For despite what he had told Master Lee, he actually wanted to learn martial arts to become a better fighter. From day one of his practice, Cheong was already plotting ways in which to use the new techniques in a fight. A few months after beginning his Chuka training, Cheong and some of his Chuka classmates had a fight with a group of boys who were saying derogatory things about the fighting art of Master Lee. Though in their minds they had an acceptable reason to fight, Master Lee scolded Cheong and his classmates and warned that if they fought again, under any circumstance, he would expel them from the school. The art and guidance of Master Lee truly changed Cheong's character, and he has not fought since.

Master Lee's Chuka Shaolin classes were held in his backyard, within easy walking distance from Cheong's home (fig 3). Classes were held seven days a week in the morning, afternoon, and evening, and each session lasted roughly two hours. Cheong was quite studious and incorrigible when it came to training. In the beginning, he trained in all three classes on each day of each week. After three or four years of consistent training, Cheong no longer had to pay the student training fee, for he became Master Lee's assistant.

Master Lee Siong Pheow died in 1961; he was seventy-seven years old. After the master's death, his disciples held a formal meeting to discuss the future of Chuka Shaolin. During this meeting one of the disciples nominated Cheong to succeed Lee as the head of the art, since it was Cheong who had learned the most from their late teacher. It was unanimously agreed. From then on, even Cheong's seniors would come to him for pointers or to learn a new technique or form.

Fig. 3

Lee Siong Pheow (seated) with his students.

Prior to Lee's passing, Cheong had never entertained the thought of teaching kung-fu for a living, and certainly not on a commercial basis. However, in 1964, with the encouragement of many people, Cheong decided to open classes in an effort to keep the art from becoming lost.

In the 1970s, Cheong opened a clothing, souvenir, and gift shop that caters to the many tourists who trek up the long stairway to the great Kwan Yin statue at the Kek Lok Si Temple, located in the Air Itam quarter of Pulau Pinang (fig. 4). After business hours, the shops and stairs empty and students gather to practice the art of Chuka Shaolin on a section of flat stone running parallel to Cheong's shop (figs. 5, 6).

Fig. 4

Fig. 5

Fig. 6

CHUKA SHAOLIN TODAY

While still obscure, the art of Chuka Shaolin has garnered somewhat of a cult following around the world. This has occurred as a result of some international exposure the art received in the early seventies through the book co-written by Cheong Cheng Leong and the late Donn F. Draeger, titled *Phoenix-Eye Fist: A Shaolin Fighting Art of South China,* and a number of articles that appeared in such magazines as *Inside Kung-Fu, Oriental Fighting Arts,* and *Martial Arts Legends.*

In 1972, Donn F. Draeger approached Cheong Cheng Leong with the prospect of the two of them writing a book together. Each year during the festival season in Penang, all of the local kung-fu clubs are invited to demonstrate their arts in public. While Draeger spent a good amount of time in Penang teaching Shindo Muso-ryu jo-jutsu, it was during the 1972 festival season that he was introduced for the first time to the dynamic fighting art of Chuka Shaolin.

Fig. 7

Not knowing Cheong personally at that time, and following the tradition of using a mediator on first introductions, especially when making a request, Donn Draeger asked an associate to introduce him to Cheong Cheng Leong. After introductions had been made, Draeger asked Cheong if he would be interested in collaborating on a book on Chuka Shaolin. Cheong was interested, but told Draeger that permission would first have to be given by Master Lee's widow and the art's senior instructors. Mrs. Lee and the seniors agreed, as long as nothing secret to the style would be revealed in print. Two or three years later, the book was written, and in 1977, it was published. Although the book had been out of print for years, with the popularity of Chinese martial arts once again on the rise, it is again available.

Aside from co-authoring that book, and the one you now hold in your hands, Cheong Cheng Leong has perpetuated the art of Chuka Shaolin through his teachings in Malaysia, Venezuela, and England. A few years ago, the Malaysian government initiated a government-sponsored Penang martial arts organization, called Malam Seni Silat Malaysia Sempena Pesta Pulau Pinang (Penang Government Kung-fu Society). All of the senior chief instructors from Penang, along with one or two from Johor, demonstrated their arts at the first gathering of the society in 1997 (fig 7).

These days Cheong Cheng Leong can still be found, several evenings a week, on the steps of the Kek Lok Si Temple imparting to a small yet dedicated group of students the dynamic and deadly art of the phoenix-eye fist: Chuka Shaolin.

CHAPTER TWO

Overview of Chuka Shaolin

As with most traditional Chinese martial arts, there is no ranking system in Chuka Shaolin; you are either a student, a teacher, or a master. Hard work and dedication are the only things that make the novice an expert and bring an expert to mastery. The hardest part for the individual interested in Chuka Shaolin, however, is not the training as much as finding a qualified and authentic teacher of this rare fighting art. Whether a teacher is found or one attempts to learn the art from a book, what is most important is to engage in proper and directed training. As one cannot learn how to run before he can walk, one cannot learn a martial art form or its fighting techniques before he has gained a strong foundation in the basics. With this in mind, this chapter outlines the training process and the four basic principles necessary to apply Chuka Shaolin for self-defense.

PROGRESSIONS IN TRAINING

Once accepted as a pupil, the first thing the novice is taught is the horse-riding stance. After this stance has been developed to a respectable degree, students are introduced to the various footwork maneuvers, including the art's unique dodging stance. The foot maneuvers are followed by hand movements, including how to form and hold the phoenix-eye fist and then how to strike with it. Once students learn how to punch, they put it together with the footwork. After a trainee has completed the fundamentals he goes on to the most basic form, *kai san,* which means "opening the mountain." The title signifies the start of the trainee's journey, a long and arduous uphill struggle. And it is only one of fifteen solo empty-hand forms to be learned.

Beginners take about one month to finish a given form before they are permitted to progress to another. Even then, they must attend three classes a week—each class lasting two hours—if they hope to do this in such a short time. Students then go on to learn another two forms, of which there are a total of twenty-five in the system: fifteen solo empty-hand forms, two two-person empty-hand forms, seven solo weapon forms, and one two-person weapon form. There are so many forms in the art because they are believed to be good for developing stamina and flexibility and for learning and developing the fighting combinations of the individual movements. After the first three empty-hand forms are learned, students move on to the two-person forms, weapons, and the fighting applications applicable therein.

In general, the Chinese method of teaching a group of students is for each student to practice on his own. When the master is free, he may come over and tell each student individually what to do. And while classes are not traditionally strict in terms of everybody being made to practice the same thing at the same time, students are not permitted to just stand around and socialize with their classmates; they must at least be sitting in a horse stance. As long as a student is doing something constructive with his training time, he can talk—permitting he is not disrupting the other students.

Practitioners of Chuka Shaolin don't train in the same militaristic fashion as do exponents of other martial arts. Generally speaking, classes are held in small, informal groups. In fact, it is believed that the only true way of perfecting a Chinese martial art is by way of private, one-on-one instruction with a master, who will teach a solo form and then a two-person form. The master will tell a student in private what each movement is only once, and then he won't show him again—the student will have to later recall it—or rediscover it—for himself. It is through this method that the diligent student will come to learn and understand the application of the forms.

As far as strength and conditioning training is concerned, in addition to the standard kung-fu sandbag, exponents of Chuka Shaolin use the phoenix-eye fist post for developing striking accuracy and conditioning of the phoenix-eye fist striking knuckle.

There are also a number of two-person arm-conditioning exercises in the art. While many styles advocate striking an inanimate object for purposes of conditioning the extremities, exponents of Chuka Shaolin believe the only way to truly develop the necessary power is to condition the arms jointly with another individual. This method of impact training develops a realistic feel of impact, distancing, body shifting and mechanics, and confidence in a close-quarter combative encounter. This type of training finds two students squaring off and banging various parts of their arms together in an effort to develop the strong forearm bones used for blocking hard strikes. Moreover, blocks are not executed force-to-force, but by way of twisting motions. As such, Chuka exponents don't feel the impact on blocking, but their opponents certainly do. So, while exponents of Chuka Shaolin use the forearms to block, such tough training occasionally injures students.

In addition to the aforementioned training methods, there are also methods of developing resistance strength, pushing and redirecting sensitivity, and pulling strength. For maximum effect, these training methods are interspersed with forms practice. The general progression is: one or two empty-hand forms, a wrist-banging exercise, a palm-up/palm-down resistance exercise, one or more empty-hand forms, push and redirect exercise, three more empty-hand forms, a pulling exercise, one more empty-hand form.

After several years of consistent training, students are introduced to chi kung internal strength and energy development exercises. These exercises are among the most important training a Chuka practitioner will engage in.

APPLYING THE ART

Chinese martial arts on the whole are an interesting lot. They are at once a physical culture, a discipline, a personal defensive system, and an art form complete with aesthetic movements and postures, poetic names for the movements and postures, and key words or phrases that both shroud and act as a mechanism through which to uncover the true meaning behind the fighting techniques.

The art of Chuka Shaolin, while being a discipline and containing poetic names for its movements, is first and foremost a pragmatic fighting art. As such, it must be immediately applicable if the art is to be of use to its exponents. There is no advantage to hidden meanings and obscured phrases in a fighting art that may need to be used at any time, especially after ten years of training. As such, the fighting theory of Chuka Shaolin is simple, direct, pragmatic, and based on the following four key principles.

Principle 1: No Unrealistic Techniques

At the basic and most fundamental level of Chuka Shaolin are methods of movement and evasion, blocking and parrying, striking and kicking. There are joint locking techniques, sweeping methods, and ground-fighting skills within the system, too. However, this training is thought to be complicated and unnecessary in gaining a basic skill in self-defense. Thus, such training is reserved for advanced students who have already learned simple and effective self-defense skills but who embrace the art and wish to develop themselves further in it. In essence, Chuka techniques are mainly applied empty-hand against empty-hand and weapon against weapon. Very little is done is terms of applying empty-hand techniques against an armed opponent.

Since the phoenix-eye fist system is a fighting art based on practicality, exponents are taught that if someone comes at them with a weapon, and they are unarmed, they should consider running—or finding a weapon of their own—rather than facing the armed opponent empty-handed. Should the opportunity permit, it is better to stack the odds in one's favor, or at least to try and balance them, than to fight a potentially losing battle.

Principle 2: Always Hit First

One of the most primal and basic of human emotions is fear. Fear is what allows one human being to be dominated by another, either physically or mentally. In terms of self-defense and fighting, fear is often the cause of improper technique, poor timing, lack of power, and hesitation. More than anything else, it is these things that will cause the practitioner to lose a fight.

During the course of their Chuka Shaolin study, students are taught to be resolute in their decision of whether they are going to fight or not. If one decides to fight, then he must fight—all out and with complete resolve. If one wants to fight, one must learn how to move fast. One mustn't think

"Oh, this guy is bigger or stronger than I and I don't know if I can beat him." If you are going to fight, go in as fast as you can and strike first with all the intention and skill you can muster.

Principle 3: Fight at Close Range

Since Chuka Shaolin is a close-range fighting art, once an opponent throws the first punch the Chuka practitioner must go in immediately. The skills of closing-the-gap or entering-in on an opponent, and remaining in the close range where the techniques of the phoenix-eye fist are most effective, are taught and developed through the practice of the two-person forms.

Exponents of Chuka Shaolin believe that their art of in-fighting and pressure-point striking is so advanced that once they close-in on an opponent, they will win. Indeed, many styles don't teach how to kick or strike effectively—and with power from such short distances—once the distance is shortened between you and your opponent. Phoenix-eye fist kung-fu excels in this range and type of fighting. The primary targets sought to be struck with the phoenix-eye fist, depending on the practitioner's position in relation to the opponent, are the sternum, ribs, throat, eyes, and temples.

Principle 4: Move to the Blind Side

The art of the phoenix-eye fist is a close-range, fast, and deceptive fighting style. Its techniques are based more on finesse of skill and precision in striking, and less on brute strength or use of force against force. As stated earlier, Chuka Shaolin exponents like to get the jump on an opponent by quickly closing the gap and moving into close range. However, if an opponent is also a skilled in-fighter, when they attempt to enter in on a Chuka practitioner, the Chuka practitioner will sidestep to the opponent's blind side, striking vital points along the side of their neck and body.

CHAPTER THREE

Fundamental Techniques

Fundamental techniques of any fighting art include various types of stances and postures, footwork and kicks, blocks and deflections, punches and strikes. Without having developed strong basics, all the timing, reflexes, and courage in the world will not win you a fight. Moreover, it is strongly developed basics that are linked together into the various solo and two-person empty-hand forms. And it is through these forms that the Chuka practitioner learns his craft.

The basic techniques of Chuka Shaolin consist of stances and postures, hand movements and techniques, foot movements and techniques, and a series of body displacements. Most of these basics have been covered in detail elsewhere; for our purposes here, we will present the basic movements that are found in the *khong shou twee chai*, or two-person fighting form. This form consists of sixteen basic techniques, which include the salutation, ready position, stances, kicks, blocks, and strikes. Following is a discussion of each of the basics found in the two-person fighting form.

STANCES AND POSTURES

There are two primary stances used within Chuka Shaolin: the horse-riding stance and the hanging-horse stance. All of the art's techniques are executed from a close range of close to medium distance from either of these stances. And while there are only two primary stances, there are variations of them and an infinite number of postures that can be formed in them. Their overall importance to the system cannot be overstated.

A stance consists of the proper placement of the legs and feet so as to "root" or connect the practitioner to the ground, thus making his base for attack and defense strong and immovable. When the stances are applied in action, as a support for movement, along with various hand and foot techniques, a great number of postures can be formed. In addition, when used in action, the stances have permutations. For example, both of the primary stances can be held while facing forward, facing left, or facing right. Depending on application, the horse-riding stance is also applied with one knee resting on the ground, thus changing the height at which a given technique can be used.

In short, stances are positions held by the feet while postures are positions of the entire body, linking stances with any number of upper-torso positions (i.e., hand and arm formations). Below is a discussion of the two primary stances, the salutation, and the ready position or fighting stance of Chuka Shaolin.

Horse-Riding Stance

The most fundamental and widely used stance in Chuka Shaolin in the horse-riding stance (fig. 1). It was given this name because the position assumed is like that of a man on horseback. While the upper body can face to either the front, right, or left, the basic stance remains the same.

Fig. 1

Horse-riding stance

To assume the horse-riding stance, begin from a natural standing position. From here, separate the feet until they are two shoulder widths apart. The precise method of "walking" into this stance is to begin with feet together and then to move the toes out and then the heels out four times, at which point the proper distance between your feet will have been reached. Once this distance has been attained, lower your center of gravity by sinking your hips. Your thighs should remain slightly higher than your knees and not end up parallel to the ground. In this position your weight should be distributed evenly over your feet and your knees should not extend past your heels.

Hanging-Horse Stance

The second stance used in Chuka Shaolin is the hanging-horse stance (fig. 2), so named because the front leg "hangs," or "floats," rather than having substantial weight resting upon it. Whereas all types of hand techniques can be employed from both the horse-riding stance and the hanging-horse stance, it is only in the latter that kicking techniques are employed. Since the front leg of the practitioner is "hanging" in this stance, it is in a prime position to launch untelegraphed and fast kicking techniques.

Fig. 2

Hanging-horse stance

To assume the hanging-horse stance, begin from a natural standing position. From here, place your weight onto either leg (in fig. 2, it's the right) and bend it at the knee slightly so as to "root" it into the ground. While doing this, lift your left leg just enough to bend it at the knee, and then slide it forward until it is one shoulder width from the right foot. Only the toes of the left foot should be touching the ground in the final position of the stance.

The Salutation

Although Chuka Shaolin is first and foremost a fighting art, its intrinsic spirit is one of self-defense. There is a certain amount of formal etiquette that each exponent of this art observes and in which the defensive spirit of the art is readily seen.

The hand sign is a characteristic form of etiquette among all exponents of Shaolin, and Chuka Shaolin is no different. Through use of a special hand sign, the Chuka exponent is able both to identify himself and to determine whether the person he meets is a genuine exponent of the Chuka art.

There are three methods of using or presenting the hand sign in Chuka Shaolin. When the Chuka hand sign is used as a greeting made in a spirit desiring no conflict with the one being greeted, the hand sign is rendered from the normal upright posture one uses when standing or walking. When facing an enemy, however, the phoenix-eye fist and spear hand configuration of the hand sign is pointing directly toward the opponent (fig. 3). And lastly, the hand sign used for demonstration or training purposes is accompanied with several additional movements so as to show respect to one's teacher, training partner, and guests. In addition, the opening and closing salutations of such demonstrations are somewhat different.

We present here only the basics of the hand sign posture, formed in a hanging-horse stance with the right hand formed in the phoenix-eye fist and the left in the spear hand positions, arms extended in front, the palm of the left hand resting on the extended knuckle of the right. The complete demonstration opening salutation is presented at the start of the pole form presented in chapter seven; the complete closing salutation is presented at the end of the two-person fighting form in chapter four.

Fig. 3

The salutation

The Ready Position

Every martial art, Chinese or otherwise, has its own ready position or fighting stance. In this art, the practitioner assumes the hanging-horse stance, which, since there is little weight on the front leg, allows the practitioner to maneuver quickly to evade an attack or to launch a quick and untelegraphed kick at his opponent (fig. 4).

In this position, the hands are held open, with the right hand extended toward the opponent at the height of the practitioner's face. This hand is used to either launch a quick strike, deflect an incoming strike, or simply protect the upper part of the torso. The left hand is held at sternum level at about the same distance from the practitioner's body as the elbow of the right arm. The left hand, then, acts as either a primary or secondary defensive mechanism, depending on what the practitioner does with his right hand. It is also used to protect the lower torso and waist area.

Fig. 4

The ready position

HAND AND FOOT MANEUVERS

The hand and foot maneuvers of Chuka Shaolin are both unique and particular. As an example, when striking and deflecting, the hands are always changing position in rapid succession, one weaving over or under the other. The opponent is given no room to mount a counteroffensive, as the Chuka Shaolin practitioner constantly strikes at vulnerable points, thus making it very difficult for an opponent to retaliate in time.

The hand maneuvers or techniques presented here are simple but effective. Indeed, they form the foundation upon which offensive and defensive fighting combinations are based. Examples of their various applications are found in the two-person fighting form that follows in the next chapter. Please note that while these techniques can be executed from either of the two primary stances, for purposes of clarity and ease of presentation, they are all demonstrated here from the horse-riding stance.

While Chuka Shaolin emphasizes hand techniques, it is a style that also makes use of a variety of different foot techniques, such as kicks, sweeps, and deflections. Chuka kicks are almost always delivered after several hand techniques have been executed, from the belief that it is best to confuse the opponent with a series of fast, interconnected hand movements first and then to follow up with fast, low kicks. Such rapid kicks to an opponent's lower extremities, unleashed after pinpoint hand strikes, are difficult to see and, therefore, nearly unstoppable.

Moreover, since exponents of Chuka Shaolin believe that high kicks are slower and more easily seen by an opponent, they concentrate their arsenal of kicks on the lower parts of the body. As such, kicks are generally aimed at the groin or knee, after which the Chuka practitioner steps in with more hand strikes to finish off an opponent.

The following twelve techniques are presented here in the order in which they are introduced in the two-person fighting form presented in the following chapter. In this way it is hoped that those interested in learning and perfecting the two-person form will have a clearer picture of what is entailed in the individual techniques and the proper placement and formation of the hands and feet within it.

Phoenix-Eye Fist Strike

Chuka Shaolin is perhaps the only martial art that exclusively uses the knuckle of the index finger (the phoenix-eye) when punching an opponent, and not the flat horizontal or vertical fist, as is the case with most other martial arts. In essence, the phoenix-eye fist strike is used to attack the body's vital points, as opposed to indiscriminate locations on the body.

This hand formation is assumed by first sitting into the horse-riding stance, with the torso held forward (fig. 5) or twisted to either the right (fig. 6) or to the left (fig. 7). The arm opposite the lead leg is extended forward and holds the phoenix-eye fist hand formation.

Fig. 5

To form the phoenix-eye fist, begin with the fingers extended and pressed together. Next, bend the bottom three fingers while leaving the index finger pointing forward. Upon fully clenching the bottom three fingers, the index finger is bent halfway, leaving the first digit protruding forward. To make the fist tighter and hence more effective, the thumb is placed over the nail of the index finger, at once pulling that finger in and pushing down on the three clenched fingers.

Fig. 6

To utilize the phoenix-eye fist strike, the fist rotates counterclockwise from vertical to diagonal prior to impact. At the same time, the opposite arm is held with palm up at a distance in front of the sternum equal to the position of the elbow of the lead arm. The rear arm serves as protection and as the chamber position for a possible follow-up strike.

The phoenix-eye fist strike is depicted here as it is applied to the front, left, and right. (figs. 5, 6, and 7) You will notice, when striking to the front, that the attacking hand is positioned off the practitioner's center line. This is done as a result of the practitioner's position in relation to the opponent: slightly off center so as not to expose his groin or vital targets running down the front of his body to his opponent.

Fig. 7

Double/Single-Palm Blocks

The double-palm block is named for its simultaneous use of the palms of both hands to block an oncoming blow (fig. 8). The single-palm block, on the other hand, is named after the use of one palm to block an oncoming blow. Whereas the single-palm block can be used to stop an average strike, the double-palm block is used when the force of an oncoming blow is great, such as that from a kick.

To utilize the double-palm block, sit into the horse-riding stance with the torso twisted either to the right or to the left (in fig. 8, to the left).

Extend both arms the same distance from the body, but do not lock the elbow at full extension. Even though both hands are extended to equal lengths, the arm in front of the practitioner's body (in this case, the right) will be closer to the opponent's body than the other hand.

Fig. 8

Lightning Kick

The lightning kick received its name because of the great speed with which the kick is executed. It is snapped out at an opponent's groin or sternum and retracted so quickly that it is difficult to see, let alone block (fig. 9).

To utilize the lightning kick, sit into a hanging-horse stance with your weight placed on the rear leg. In this position, there is little weight on the front foot, making the time necessary to launch the kick less than if you first had to transfer your weight onto the supporting leg, as would happen if you attempted to kick from the horse-riding stance. From the hanging-horse stance, raise your thigh slightly so that it is parallel to the ground;

then, in a single motion, snap out the ball of your foot from the knee straight into your opponent's sternum or groin and retract it.

Please note that as the kick is launched forward, the opposite arm (in fig 9, the left arm) is held palm down near the kicking knee, while the same arm as the kicking leg is lowered. In this way, the Chuka Shaolin practitioner not only harnesses the most power he can from his kick through counterbalancing, but he is also in a position to be able to quickly and effectively block or deflect his opponent's counterattack should one come while he is kicking.

Fig. 9

Double Dragon Two-Finger Strike

The double dragon two-finger strike is so named because the hands, when formed with the index and middle fingers protruding forward from an otherwise clenched fist, resemble the tails of two dragons ready to simultaneously strike at an opponent's eyes (fig. 10).

Fig. 10

To utilize the double dragon two-finger strike, sit into the horse-riding stance with the torso twisted to either the right or the left (in this case, to the right). The arm matching the lead leg (the right arm, here), the defensive arm, is held lower than the arm matching the rear leg (the left arm).

When striking, the fist of the left, or attacking, arm—formed with the index and middle fingers protruding and pointing toward the opponent—is thrust forward at the opponent's eyes. Be sure not to lock the elbow on impact, or injury may occur. Concurrent with the execution of this technique, the defensive arm (the right arm) is held with palm up at a distance in front of the sternum equal to the position of the elbow of the lead arm (the left). The rear arm serves as protection and as the chamber position for a possible follow-up block or strike.

Upper-Palm Block

The upper-palm block is so named because you both block an oncoming strike with the palm of the upper (or higher) of your two hands and also because you direct your opponent's strike upward with your palm on impact (fig. 11).

To utilize the upper-palm block, sit into the horse-riding stance with the torso twisted either to the right or to the left (in our example, to the left). The arm matching the lead leg (the left arm, here) is held lower than the arm matching the rear leg (in this case, the right arm). When blocking, the palm of your rear hand (the right) meets the underside of your opponent's oncoming strike and lifts it upward in the hopes of not only redirecting the block but also exposing his weak points in the process. Concurrent with the execution of this technique, the defensive arm (in this case, the left arm) is held with palm up at a distance in front of the sternum equal to the position of the elbow of the lead arm. The rear arm serves as protection and as the chamber position for a possible follow-up block or strike.

Middle-Palm Block

The middle-palm block received its name because of the location of the body along which the block is utilized: the middle or midsection. The middle-palm block is similar to the upper-palm block in that the palm of one hand is used to block and redirect an opponent's oncoming strike. However, rather than using the palm to redirect the strike upward, it is used to send the strike downward (fig. 12).

Fig. 12

To utilize the middle-palm block, sit into the horse-riding stance facing forward. Depending on what position you were in prior to executing the block and the position of your opponent's strike, either hand may be used to block. For our example, the right arm is used to demonstrate the technique. As such, when blocking, the palm of your right hand meets the top of your opponent's oncoming strike and thrusts it downward in the hopes of not only redirecting the blow but also exposing several of your opponent's vulnerable targets in the process. While executing this technique, the defensive arm (in this case, the left arm) is held with palm up at a distance in front of the sternum equal to the position of the elbow of the lead arm. The defensive arm serves as both protection and as the chamber position for a possible follow-up block or strike.

Thrust-Penetrate-Tear Hand

The thrust-penetrate-tear hand received its name because of the many uses of this complex technique. In essence, this technique uses a thrusting action, a penetrating action, and a tearing action, depending on the circumstance. Regardless of its ultimate usage, the hand is thrust out toward an opponent with fingers and wrist extended and pointing down (fig. 13).

To utilize the thrust-penetrate-tear hand, sit into the horse-riding stance with the torso twisted either to the right or to the left (to the left, here). The arm matching the lead leg (in this case, the left arm) is held directly behind the attacking arm (in this case, the right arm). When executing this technique, your attacking hand is thrust in spearlike fashion to a vital spot on your opponent's body, at which point it grabs and pulls or tears the location using a clawlike motion. While executing this technique, the defensive arm (in this case, the left arm) is held with palm up at a distance in front of the sternum equal to the position of the elbow of the lead arm. The rear arm serves as both protection and as the chamber position for a possible follow-up block or strike.

Fig. 13

Upper-Wrist Block

The upper-wrist block is so named because of the blocking action of the technique, which is done with the top of the wrist (fig. 14). Since this blocking method is most effective when used against frontal kicking actions such as the lightning kick and the heart-penetrating kick, it is necessary to drop your center of gravity to get underneath the attack.

To utilize the upper-wrist block, sit into the horse-riding stance with the torso twisted either to the right or to the left (in our example, to the left) and drop down to one knee (in this case, the right knee). The arm matching the lead leg (the left arm) is held directly behind the blocking arm (the right arm). When blocking, it is necessary to keep the fingers together and bend the wrist down, so as to expose the wrist and strengthen the wrist/forearm connection. The upper side of your wrist is used for blocking and meets the underside of your opponent's oncoming kick and lifts it upward in the hopes of not only redirecting the kick but also exposing his weak points in the process. While executing this technique, the defensive arm (in this case, the left arm) is held with palm up at a distance in front of the sternum equal to the position of the elbow of the lead arm. The rear arm serves as both protection and as the chamber position for a possible follow-up block or strike.

Fig. 14

High and Middle-Wrist Block

The high and middle-wrist block is so named because of the simultaneous high and mid-level blocking actions performed with the wrists of both hands (fig. 15). This blocking method is used against various two-handed strikes and is also used when the Chuka Shaolin practitioner is unsure as to the exact location of an oncoming strike, in effect simultaneously protecting all areas of his body.

Fig. 15

To utilize the high and middle-wrist block, sit into the horse-riding stance facing forward. Depending on what position you were in prior to executing the block, and depending on your opponent's strike, either hand may be used to block either high or to the middle. For our example, the right arm is defending the high line while the left is used to defend the middle line. Both hands are maneuvered clockwise, circling from the inside out, to meet the oncoming strike with the wrist area of the arms. At the completion of the block, the right hand is held palm up and is the closer of the two arms to your opponent: the left hand is held palm down and is farther away from the opponent.

Double Phoenix-Eye Fist Strike

The double phoenix-eye fist strike received its name because of the simultaneous phoenix-eye fist striking action, using both right and left hands and striking both high and low (figs. 16–17). In general, the lead hand strikes low while the other hand strikes high, so as to maintain a better sense of balance. As with all of the Chuka Shaolin techniques, the situation ultimately dictates which is the lead hand at any given time.

To utilize the double phoenix-eye fist strike, sit into the horse-riding stance facing forward. Both hands, formed into phoenix-eye fists, are crossed at your center. The arm matching the lead leg (in this case, the right) is held in front. From this position, move the lead leg forward into a horse-riding stance while simultaneously punching forward with both hands, thus executing a double phoenix-eye fist strike.

Fig. 16

Fig. 17

Low Block

The low block is so named because of the height of the attacks it is used to block. In essence, it is a defensive movement used to block oncoming blows to the lower extremities of the body (fig. 18). This is generally performed while in transition from one stance to the next, particularly while attempting to change the distance between or your position in reference to an opponent.

The low block is generally performed out of the horse-riding stance while turning 180 degrees in an attempt to block a strike and reposition oneself. As shown here, pivot your torso and feet 180 degrees from a left lead horse-riding stance, ending with legs crossed. During this turning motion it is important to turn your head first so as to always keep a visual lock on your opponent. It is essential that on the completion of the turn your hand is in position in line with your hips to block your opponent's strike. In essence, the rear hand becomes the front or blocking hand at the completion of the turn (in this case, the right hand). At the same time, your other hand is placed, with palm facing your opponent, in front of your neck to protect the upper areas of your body and to launch a counterstrike of your own, should the situation dictate.

Fig. 18

CHAPTER FOUR

Two-Person Fighting Form

Traditionally speaking, there is no sparring practice in Chinese martial arts. Indeed, the techniques are thought to be too deadly, and the art held so sacred as a means of self-defense, that to bring it into a sportive arena would be no less than to degenerate the art. Moreover, in Chuka Shaolin, the main anatomical weapon used for striking is the phoenix-eye fist, a hand formation targeted at the body's most vital points. As a result, a practitioner cannot properly demonstrate or perform the movements, but must instead hold back. Thus, it is believed that it is better to go all-out in pre-arranged fighting sequences than to execute techniques in an improper fashion, as would occur in a competitive sparring setting.

Purpose of Two-Person Forms

In essence, two-person forms are invaluable when practicing the fighting techniques learned in the solo fist forms. By doing this, the practitioner learns how to perform the individual movements properly, how to connect those movements into fighting combinations, and then how to counter the movements. In addition to learning proper distancing and timing, the practice of two-person forms also hardens practitioners' courage so they won't be afraid when facing an opponent at close range. Indeed, when practicing these sets, you must punch your partner with the intention of actually hitting him and not missing. Each partner, then, soon becomes skilled enough in the art as to be able to realistically block oncoming strikes. After all, if a practitioner cannot block, deflect, or avoid a techniques in a prearranged, two-person set, then he certainly won't be able do so in a real-life self-defense situation.

It is best for new students to always practice and perform the two-person forms with the same person. When you change partners the form also changes, as your speed and distance will be different. Of course, if you are attacked on the street, your opponent will not be as cooperative as your training partner. Fighting is an entirely different story. So, for training and demonstration purposes, it is preferable to always have the same partner. For fighting purposes, one should train with different partners all of the time.

It is said that to practice a solo empty-hand form is to know yourself, but to practice a two-person form is to know your opponent. In real combative encounters, it is necessary to truly know both oneself and one's enemy. With this in mind, await the first movement with quietness of mind, a solid spirit within, and a show of ease on the outside without betraying either your feelings or intentions. When the other party attacks, whether quickly or slowly, you will meet him in the same manner, thereby striking only after the enemy has struck and in time with him.

Once the basics are developed and the solo empty-hand forms well-performed, the Chuka practitioner goes on to practice the same movements again—but this time against a partner. At this point, all the basics come together into immediately identifiable combinations of combative techniques. Which techniques work well in combination with others? How fast can you truly move from one position to another in the face of danger? How much time do you realistically have to react between attacks and counters? These are the things that are brought out and realized through the practice of the two-person fighting forms. And it is at this stage of training that the Chuka practitioner, if he is intuitive and analytical, will come to truly understand the connection between himself and his opponent, between himself and his art, between his art and his opponent.

What follows is the first of two two-person fighting forms found in Chuka Shaolin, known simply as *khong shou twee chai,* or empty-hand sparring. For purposes of simplicity and for ease in presenting the form here, it is broken down into five sections. When performed for training or demonstration, the sections should be executed in succession, one after the other, without a break in timing, speed, or intention. In addition, in an effort to aid the reader in determining the correct timing and linking of movements, the photographic descriptions have been broken down in terms of linked sequences of movements. For clarity of instruction, the partners here are named A and B, with the person initiating the form on the left as A and the person on the right as B.

BREAKDOWN OF THE FORM

Part One

Both partners begin the two-person fighting form by facing each other in a left lead ready position (fig. 1). A initiates the form by stepping forward with his right leg into a horse-riding stance and attacking B with a left-hand phoenix-eye fist strike to the solar plexus. To block the oncoming strike, B pivots to his left, moving into a horse-riding stance, and employs a middle-palm block (fig. 2).

Fig. 1

Fig. 2

B initiates an attack by stepping forward with his right leg into a horse-riding stance and attacking A with a left-hand phoenix-eye fist strike to the solar plexus (fig. 3). To block the oncoming strike, A pivots to his left, moving into a horse-riding stance, and employs a middle-palm block (fig. 4).

Fig. 3

Fig. 4

A then launches a lightning kick at B, who pivots to his left, moving into a horse-riding stance, and blocks a single-palm block (fig. 4).

Fig. 5

Fig. 6

B then launches a lightning kick at A, who pivots to his left, moving into a horse-riding stance, and blocks with a middle-palm block (fig. 5).

Fig. 7

Fig. 8

Part Two

A and B then step back into a left lead ready position (fig. 6). B steps forward into a left lead horse-riding stance and launches a three-strike hand combination, consisting of a double dragon two-finger strike with his right hand at A's eyes, a phoenix-eye fist strike with his left hand to A's sternum, and a thrust-penetrate-tear hand strike with his right hand to A's groin. In his defense, A creates the necessary distance by stepping back with his right leg into a horse-riding stance, blocking with an upper-palm block, and a right and then left middle block (figs. 7–9).

Fig. 9

Fig. 10

Fig. 11

Fig. 12

A and B then step back into left lead ready position (fig. 10). The previous sequence then repeats itself on the opposite side, wherein A steps forward into a right lead horse-riding stance and launches a three-strike hand combination, consisting of a double dragon two-finger strike with his left hand at B's eyes, a phoenix-eye fist strike with his right hand to B's sternum, and a thrust-penetrate-tear hand strike with his left hand to B's groin. In his defense, B creates the necessary distance by stepping back with his left leg into a horse-riding stance, blocking with an upper-palm block, and a right and then left middle-palm block (figs. 11–13).

Fig. 13

Fig. 14

Fig. 15

Fig. 16

Part Three

A and B both step back into a left lead ready position (fig. 14). B launch-es a three-strike combination, this time while advancing forward, consisting of a phoenix-eye fist strike to A's sternum with his left hand, a phoenix-eye fist strike to A's sternum with his right hand, and a right lightning kick to A's midsection. In his defense, A first pivots to his left and employs a dou-ble-palm block, then he pivots to his right and employs another double-palm block, and then he changes into a right lead hanging-horse stance while employing a single-palm block (figs. 15–17). A and B both step back into a left lead ready position (fig. 18).

The sequence then repeats on the opposite side. This time, A launches a three-strike combination while advancing forward, consisting of a phoenix-eye fist strike to B's sternum with his left hand, a phoenix-eye fist strike to B's sternum with his right hand, and a right lightning kick to B's midsection. In his defense, B first pivots to his left and employs a double-palm block, then he pivots to his right and employs another double-palm block, and then he changes into a right lead hanging-horse stance while employing a single-palm block (figs. 19–21).

Fig. 17

Fig. 18

Fig. 19

Fig. 20

Fig. 21

Fig. 22

Fig. 23

Fig. 24

A and B both step back into a left lead ready position (fig. 22). A steps forward into a right horse-riding stance and attacks B with a double phoenix-eye fist strike, which B blocks by moving his right leg sideways to assume a horse-riding stance and blocking with a high and low block (figs. 23–24). A follows this by retracting his right leg until it is parallel with his left and launching a right- and then left-hand phoenix-eye fist strike combination to B's sternum, which B blocks by first pivoting to his right and then to his left, utilizing a double-palm block in his defense (figs. 25–27). Sensing an opening in A's defense, B immediately follows his block by stepping forward with his right leg and countering with a left and then right phoenix-eye fist strike combination, which A blocks with a right and then a left low-block combination immediately followed with a right jump lightning kick (figs. 28–33).

Fig. 25

Fig. 26

Fig. 27

Fig. 28

Fig. 29

Fig. 30

Fig. 31

Fig. 32

Fig. 33

Fig. 34

Fig. 35

Fig. 36

Part Four

A and B both step back into a left lead ready position (fig. 34). B then steps forward into a right horse-riding stance and attacks A with a double phoenix-eye fist strike, which A blocks by moving his left leg sideways to assume a horse-riding stance and blocking with a high and low block (figs. 35–36). B follows this by stepping forward with his left leg until it is parallel with his right and launching a right- and then left-hand phoenix-eye fist strike combination to A's sternum, which A blocks by first pivoting to his right and then to his left, utilizing a double-palm block in his defense (figs. 37–39). Sensing an opening in B's defense, A immediately follows his block by stepping forward with his right leg and countering with a left- and then right-hand phoenix-eye fist strike combination, which B blocks with a right and then a left low-block combination, which B immediately follows with a right jump lightning kick (figs. 40–44).

Fig. 37

Fig. 38

Fig. 39

Fig. 40

Fig. 41

Fig. 42

Fig. 43

Fig. 44

Part Five

A and B both step back into a left lead ready position (fig. 45). B attacks with a right lightning kick to A's midsection, which A blocks by moving his right leg out into a horse-riding stance and utilizing an upper-wrist block (fig. 46). A immediately follows this with a right lightning kick of his own to B's midsection, which B blocks by pivoting to his left and dropping down on his right knee and utilizing an upper-wrist block (figs. 47–48). A and B both step back into a left lead ready position (fig. 49) then launch simultaneous right-hand phoenix-eye fist strikes at each other's sternum

Fig. 45

Fig. 46

Fig. 47

(fig. 50). Thus ends the fighting section of the form. The two-person fight-ing form is concluded with the formal salutation from left hanging-horse stances, wherein they simultaneously extend their left arms toward the ground and their right arms toward the sky, then, with hands formed in the phoenix-eye fist hand sign, they first pull their hands to their left hip and then extend it forward (figs. 51–53). After they have saluted one another, A and B turn to face the teachers, judges, or guests who might be present, and offer their respects with the hand sign (fig. 54).

Fig. 48

Fig. 49

Fig. 50

Fig. 51

Fig. 52

Fig. 53

Fig. 54

Conditioning and Strength Exercises

Conditioning and strength exercises play an important role in Chuka Shaolin training. It is these exercises that harden the weak parts of the limbs used for blocking and striking, in essence making them as hard as iron. In times past, exponents of various martial arts around the world used to toughen their entire bodies—all parts of the hands, wrists, forearms, stomachs, shins, head, and so on—until they were impervious to pain and thus unaffected by an opponent's blows. Over time, however, more precise and scientific fighting arts developed, emphasizing dynamic mobility, fast body movement, efficient deflections and blocks, and precise striking skills. Thus, over-conditioning of the body became unnecessary.

CONDITIONING EXERCISES

Chuka Shaolin evolved along these lines, and is of the philosophy that it is only necessary to "toughen" or condition the few specific parts of the body that are used for impacting an opponent and are not otherwise protected. As such, it is only the knuckle of the phoenix-eye fist and the wrists that are hardened through conditioning exercises. As for the other parts of the anatomy, since the art is precise as to its target, the soft parts of the hands, used only to impact on soft parts of an opponent's body, such as the eyes, throat, and neck, are not conditioned while the feet are generally covered with a shoe of some sort. Thus, such an exaggeration of body conditioning is viewed as unnecessary.

Post-Striking Exercise

The primary strike used in Chuka Shaolin is the phoenix-eye fist. It is not surprising, then, that a mechanism developed through which to not only toughen the knuckle of the phoenix-eye fist but to concurrently train the exponent's target selection and accuracy. That mechanism is the one- and five-target striking pads.

There are two striking posts used for training in Chuka Shaolin: the first consists of five, one-inch-thick rubber pads mounted on a wooden frame connected to two mounted wooden posts. The second consists of a single, one-inch rubber pad mounted to a single post. Both types of posts are planted in the ground. Whereas the single-pad post is useful for developing target accuracy and conditioning, the five-pad post can train these things as well as target selection and footwork.

As can be see from the accompanying photograph (fig. 1), the original training posts have deteriorated over time as a result of overuse and the dry rot so common in the tropical climate of Malaysia. These days, students prefer to condition their phoenix-eye fist by striking the generic yet highly popular canvas sand bags.

Fig. 1

For clarity of illustration, we have mounted the five pads to a white wall so that the reader will be better able to follow the striking sequence. Please note, however, that you cannot strike pads mounted to a wall with the same force as you can pads mounted to wooden posts. Posts offer a certain amount of "give" when struck, thus reducing chances of injury; a solid wall does not.

Regardless of whether you chose to train with the traditional padded posts or with sand bags, the five targets should be arranged as follows: three pads running in a straight, vertical line, and two pads placed parallel to each other on either side of the vertical line and between the bottom two pads (fig. 2). The targets that these pads represent are as follows: the uppermost pad is the space between the eyes known as the "third eye"; the middle pad is the throat; the bottom pad can be the sternum or groin; the leftmost pad is the right floating rib; and the rightmost pad is the left floating rib. It is important to keep in mind that the height and location of these targets is approximate, as such things are necessarily dictated by the size of a Chuka Shaolin exponent in relation to the height of an opponent.

Fig. 2

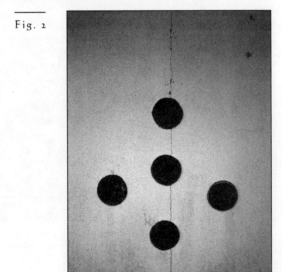

Begin the striking sequence from a right lead ready position (fig. 3). Advance forward with the right leg into a horse-riding stance while extending the right hand, simulating a block or protective position (fig. 4); next, execute three consecutive phoenix-eye fist strikes to the three vertical pads: the left hand strikes the upper pad (fig. 5), the right hand strikes the middle pad (fig. 6), and the left hand strikes the lowermost pad (fig. 7). From here, shift your body to the left and execute a right phoenix-eye fist strike to the leftmost pad (fig. 8); next, shift your body to the right and execute a left phoenix-eye fist strike to the leftmost pad (fig. 9).

Fig. 3

Fig. 4

Fig. 5

Fig. 6

Fig. 7

Fig. 8

Fig. 9

At this point, the striking sequence has been completed on one side only. In the interest of having balanced techniques, it is necessary to complete the sequence from the opposite lead. So, from the last position above, step back into a left lead ready position, and begin the sequence again, this time with the opposite lead and beginning with a right phoenix-eye fist strike. Note that this time around the two side strikes will be executed first to the right and then to the left. After completion of the sequence, step back again into a right lead ready position and repeat the entire sequence as many times as you like.

Wrist-Banging Exercise

The wrist-banging exercise was developed as a means of hardening and toughening the wrist bones in an effort to not only reduce the pain felt when blocking but also to have the ability to inflict injury to an opponent's limbs as a result of a hard and powerful blocking action. Aside from conditioning the wrists, this exercise also teaches how to protect the solar plexus area while moving, as well as how to absorb the shock of a hard blow on impact while staying firmly rooted in stance and without losing balance.

Begin the exercise by facing your partner in a horse-riding stance and swinging your right hand, palm up, clockwise from the inside out, wrists impacting at the completion of the motion (fig. 10). This is followed by swinging your right hand, with fist clenched, counterclockwise down, wrists impacting at the completion of the motion (fig. 11). Next, pivot your upper body to the right and swing your left hand, palm up, counterclockwise from the inside out, wrists impacting at the completion of the motion (fig. 12). This is followed by swinging your left hand, with fist clenched, clockwise down, wrists impacting at the completion of the motion (fig. 13).

Fig. 10

Fig. 11

Fig. 12

Fig. 13

From this position, the partner on the right takes one step forward with his left leg as the partner on the left takes one step backward with his right leg. Each partner simultaneously swings his right hand, palm up, clockwise from the inside out, wrists impacting at the completion of the motion (fig. 14). This is followed by swinging the right hand, with fist clenched, counterclockwise down, wrists impacting at the completion of the motion (fig. 15). Next, the partner on the right takes one step forward with his right leg as the partner on the left takes one step backward with his right leg. Each partner simultaneously swings his left hand, palm up, counterclockwise from the inside out, wrists impacting at the completion of the motion (fig. 16). This is followed by swinging the left hand, with fist clenched, clockwise down, wrists impacting at the completion of the motion (fig. 17). Next, the partner on the right takes one step forward with his left leg as the partner on the left takes one step backward with his right leg, while simultaneously swinging the right hand, palm up, clockwise from the inside out, wrists impacting at the completion of the motion (fig. 18). This is followed by swinging the right hand, with fist clenched, counterclockwise down, wrists impacting at the completion of the motion (fig. 19).

Fig. 14

Fig. 15

Fig. 16

Fig. 17

Fig. 18

Fig. 19

This sequence is repeated another three times, this time finding the partner on the left advancing three times and the partner on the right retreating three times. From the previous position, the partner on the left takes one step forward with his right leg as the partner on the right takes one step backward with his left leg. Each partner simultaneously swings the left hand, palm up, counterclockwise from the inside out, wrists impacting at the completion of the motion (fig.20). This is followed by swinging the left hand, with fist clenched, clockwise down, wrists impacting at the completion of the motion (fig. 21). Next, the partner on the left takes one step forward with his left leg as the partner on the right takes one step backward with his right leg. Each partner simultaneously swings his right hand, palm up, clockwise from the inside out, wrists impacting at the completion of the motion (fig. 22). This is followed by swinging the right hand, with fist clenched, counterclockwise down, wrists impacting at the completion of the motion (fig. 23). Next, the partner on the left takes one step forward with his right leg as the partner on the right takes one step backward with his left leg. Each partner simultaneously swings the left hand, palm up, counterclockwise from the inside out, wrists impacting at the completion of the motion (fig. 24). This is followed by swinging the left hand, with fist clenched, clockwise down, wrists impacting at the completion of the motion (fig. 25).

Fig. 20

Fig. 21

Fig. 22

Fig. 23

Fig. 24

Fig. 25

In sum, the wrist-banging exercise consists of inside and outside wrist strikes, with both right and left arms, while utilizing body shifting and advancing and retreating steps. Each repetition of the exercise is made up of high and low wrist-impacting blows from a parallel leg horse-riding stance followed by high and low wrist-impacting blows with three forward and three backward steps. Thus, a total of sixteen movements makes up one set. Each part of the exercise should be repeated at least three times, but may be performed as many times as one desires.

Upon completion of the exercise, regardless of how many times it has been performed, it is necessary to rub and massage the wrists and forearms so as to promote blood circulation, relaxation, and reduce the trauma to the area, thus speeding recovery time.

STRENGTH EXERCISES

Exponents of Chuka Shaolin believe in the importance of having strong bodies and in developing strength in various types of pushing and pulling motions, so as to hit harder, block with more stability, and have stronger overall techniques. Since Chuka Shaolin is a practical martial art, it is concerned with developing strength without the use of equipment or large spaces. It is along these lines that there developed a series of partner strength training exercises. Following is a presentation of the three core strength training exercises used in Chuka Shaolin.

Pushing Exercise

The pushing exercise is used as a means of developing a solid and forceful palm push or strike as well as the proper body structure and mechanics necessary to deflect such a blow.

The partners begin the pushing exercise by sitting into a left lead horse-riding stance with right arms extended in front and touching at the back of the wrists (fig. 26). The partner on the right moves first by attempting to push forward with his right hand and strike his partner's chest, which the partner on the left redirects by keeping his right arm secure and turning his hips to the right (fig. 27). From here, the partner on the left attempts to push forward with his right hand and strike his partner's chest (fig. 28), which the partner on the right redirects by keeping his right arm secure and turning his hips to the right (fig. 29). The partners then move back to the starting position (fig. 30) and repeat the sequence again.

Fig. 26

Fig. 27

Fig. 28

Fig. 29

Fig. 30

In sum, the pushing exercise consists of one partner pushing while the other pulls or redirects the oncoming push. Each repetition of the exercise is made up of two movements—a push and a redirection—performed by each partner. Each exercise should be repeated at least three times but may be performed as many times as one desires.

Isometric Strength Exercise

Isometric, or resistance, training is nothing new to the martial arts and has been utilized in innumerable forms by kung-fu practitioners over the centuries. The use of the specific isometric strength exercise used in Chuka Shaolin is threefold: offering a means of simultaneously developing extraordinary grip strength, pushing down strength, and lifting up strength. Whereas solid grip strength gives one the ability to securely latch onto an opponent, the development of pushing down and lifting up strength offers the practitioner options for moving an opponent once a tight grip has been secured.

The isometric strength exercise is performed in two parts. Begin the first part by securely gripping the underside of your partner's left wrist. In this position, your left hand will be both gripping and on top of your partner's right hand, and you will both be in a right lead hanging-horse stance (fig. 31). From this position, one partner holds his hands firm while the other pushes down with his left hand and up with his right hand (fig. 32). The partners then switch roles as the one who held firm now pushes and lifts while the one who had pushed and pulled remains firm.

Fig. 31

The second part of the exercise is performed the way as the first, but with each partner's right hands gripping the underside of the other's left wrist, and while assuming a left lead horse-riding stance (fig. 33).

It is sufficient to just push/lift for a moment, then relax, and then to push/lift again. In this way you get maximum effects from the exercise without fatiguing the arms with prolonged pushing, resulting in a negative return on effort exerted. There is no limit to how many times you may perform the exercise, as long as both arms and partners are given equal training time.

Fig. 32

Fig. 33

Pulling Exercise

Once the Chuka exponent has developed sufficient gripping, pushing, and lifting strength, he goes on to develop pulling strength. Although the primary purpose of this exercise is to develop pulling strength and dynamic balance when pulling and when being pulled, it is within the exercise that all of the aforementioned strength types come into play.

The partners begin this pulling exercise by facing each another in parallel horse-riding stances. The partner on the right initiates by extending his left arm forward. The partner on the left then grabs the wrist of the extended arm with his left hand and begins to pull the arm just enough so as to then place his right hand on the shoulder of the extended arm. Once this position has been achieved, the partner on the left pulls and pushes the arm down by turning his waist to the left, retracting his left hand, and pushing down on the shoulder with his right hand (fig. 34). From this position, the partner on the right then tries to counter the movement, regain his balance, and reverse the situation by pulling his left arm back to the center (fig. 35).

Once he has successfully regained his balance and pulled his opponent's arm to the center, he then grabs the wrist of the opponent's extended arm with his left hand and places his right hand on the shoulder of the extended arm. Once this position has been achieved, the partner on the right pulls and pushes the arm down by turning his waist to the left, retracting his left hand, and pushing down on the shoulder with his right hand (fig. 36).

Since the purpose of this exercise is to develop dynamic strength and balance when pulling and while being pulled, you may sometimes find it necessary to adjust your stance a bit in order to effect the pulling technique.

Fig. 34

Fig. 35

Fig. 36

CHAPTER SIX

Overview of Chuka Shaolin Weapons

Different systems of kung-fu use different types and styles of weapons. Since Chuka Shaolin is a southern Chinese martial art, and the people of that region are for the most part farmers, the style makes use of the farmer's hoe and iron rulers (truncheon). In total, Chuka Shaolin makes use of five weapons: the pole, long spear, iron rulers, twin knives, and farmer's hoe (fig. 1). At one time the art also included the nine-section steel whip. However, its use has been lost over time.

The five weapons contain four basic movements each and at least one solo form—although the pole and long spear have two solo forms each. In addition, the pole has a two-person fighting form, whereas the other weapons do not.

Fig. 1

Chuka students must train for at least one year in the empty-hand art before they are introduced to weapons training. When they do begin their weapons training, the first weapon they are introduced to is the *koon*, or pole. It takes approximately one month to complete the first koon form, known as the six-and-a-half-point pole, after which the student may be introduced to the two-person fighting pole form.

THE POLE: CHUKA SHAOLIN'S PRIMARY WEAPON

In days past, the masters of Chuka Shaolin always brought a koon along with them when they went looking for herbs in the forest. They would use the koon to scare away the wild animals and snakes whose paths they crossed while collecting herbs, and then use it as a carrying pole to transport the herbs in containers hanging off the ends of the pole, which was held across the shoulders.

As a young boy, Cheong Cheng Leong used to see a lot of farmers carrying their vegetables on the poles to the village market. They even formed a group called the Red Towel Gang to protect themselves from those intent on robbing them of their hard-earned crop. These farmers were quite famous in their time in the Air Itam area of Penang. In fact, it is said that over time few gangsters dared to attack them, as the farmers would all band together and fight using their poles.

The measurement of the practitioner's pole is set to the individual height of the practitioner, and extends roughly eighteen inches above the head. In Chuka Shaolin, the koon is held with both hands toward one end. This type of pole use is referred to as the "single headed" pole (fig. 2). Depending on distance and application, it may be necessary to sometimes use the butt end of the pole for striking.

For good balance and issuance of power, the diameter of each end of the single-headed koon should be different—the pole should be tapered. One end should be about three centimeters, while the other should be about two centimeters.

Fig. 2

The koon should not be so long as to affect its maneuverability, thus posing a danger if the opponent moves in or if a location is too small. Furthermore, the end power is minimized if the koon is too long and one can easily feel its heaviness and quickly tire. It is important that a practitioner be able to

deliver or transmit his power *(chin)* to the end point of the koon. It is equal-
ly important that the practitioner learn to deliver strikes with the tip of the
koon with accuracy and precision (figs. 3 and 4). These days, however, many
kung-fu exponents do not emphasize accuracy since it requires a lot of training and concentration. This lack of emphasis has occurred as the use of such
a long and heavy weapon is not so much in favor these days, coupled with
mainland China's promotion of the modern *wushu*, which relies more on
aesthetic beauty and grace (although some of the modern wushu pole per-
formers are quite powerful in their movements).

Fig. 3

Fig. 4

The quality of the material used for making the koon is also important. For purposes of training, a heavier pole can and should be used, as it helps the practitioner improve grip strength, body mechanics, and striking power. When using a pole for demonstration or for combat, it is advisable to use a lighter, stronger, and springier wood. And while it is relatively easy to acquire good wood in China, in Malaysia it is rather difficult. In order to get the lightness and springiness desired, Chuka practitioners in Malaysia must use rattan, which, although more flexible than the Chinese wood, can actually be a hindrance to the single-headed koon holders while performing their skills.

After the solo and two-person pole forms have been perfected, students have a choice of which weapon they will learn next. Getting to this stage takes time, at least two or three years of dedicated training. In fact, many students, even if they practice a weapon over a prolonged period, generally don't practice diligently. As a result, when asked to demonstrate the form, they are found to be below par. For this reason, among others, weapons forms and weapons training are not stressed in the Chuka Shaolin curriculum of today. If, on the other hand, a student is hardworking and diligent, he may be taught another weapon form in as little as two or three months. However, the fighting applications of the weapons are not taught until the basic movements and forms of the weapons have been mastered.

SECONDARY WEAPONS

Of secondary importance with regard to Chuka Shaolin's weapon art is the use of the long spear, iron rulers, twin knives, and farmer's hoe. Though defending one's property with farm weapons is no longer a way of life, and people do not generally walk down the street with a long spear or twin knives at their side, it is evident why such weapons rank second in importance to the pole—the skills of which are immediately applicable with any length object. However, in terms of perpetuating a martial culture and art form, the aforementioned weapons are still included in the Chuka Shaolin curriculum, and readily taught to students who have developed skills in the empty-hand art and with the pole.

Long Spear

The long spear is among the traditional weapons of Chinese martial arts and is maneuvered in essentially the same way as the pole (fig. 5). Like the pole, it is held at one end with both hands. Unlike the pole, its primary function is as a thrusting weapon, as opposed to an impacting weapon. As such, the maneuvering of the long spear is quite fast and elusive as its center is used for blocking and redirecting an oncoming blow, thus creating an opening for a deadly thrust of its point. Around the top of the spear and just below the spear point is a bushel of red tassel (fig. 6). This is used both for temporarily confusing or blinding an opponent and for entangling his spear point, should the opponent be using such a weapon.

Fig. 5

Fig. 6

Iron Rulers

The iron rulers or truncheon is another traditional Chinese weapon that stems from a farming tool (figs. 7 and 8). As a truncheon, it is used to make holes in the ground for purposes of planting. As a weapon, it became popular in Okinawa, where it is known as the *sai*. Iron rulers are used in pairs and are constructed of three pieces of metal: a long straight rod and two smaller curved pieces that separate the handle from the weapon. These protrusions act as a mechanism in which to capture an opponent's weapon for a moment, thus rendering him susceptible to a counterattack. Since the iron rulers are somewhat small, they are used in unison when blocking oncoming weapons, wherein on impact they separate, one redirecting the opponent's weapon and one striking the opponent.

Twin Knives

The twin knives are a weapon popular among southern Chinese fighting arts. They consist of two long knives of equal length and constructed of steel. Below the steel blade, which curves at the point, is a handle with a half-circle of steel running directly below the blade's edge (figs. 9 and 10).

This is used to protect the twin knife wielder's hands from an opponent's weapon should that weapon slide down the blade. Like the iron rulers, the twin knives have a length of steel curving up from the handle and alongside the blade's blunt side, which is used to momentarily entrap an opponent's weapon, thus making him susceptible to a counterattack. Also like the iron rulers, the twin knives are generally used in unison when blocking, in a block, redirect, and counterdefensive method.

Fig. 7

Fig. 8

Fig. 9

Fig. 10

Fig. 11

Fig. 12

Farmer's Hoe

The farmer's hoe is constructed of a length of wood with a sharp, flattened piece of steel at one end (figs. 11 and 12). The farmer's hoe is handled and maneuvered in much the same way as the pole and the long spear; however, it possesses the unique ability to not only hit and thrust but to also hack down on an opponent. Because of the metal protruding a few inches below the tip of the pole, the Chuka Shaolin exponent is able to inflict serious injury upon his opponent's limbs and head by merely lowering the weapon. Although not a very popular kung-fu weapon nowadays, the farmer's hoe certainly has its place in the overall skills developed by exponents of Chuka Shaolin.

The Six-and-a-Half-Point Pole Form

This chapter presents the first prearranged solo form for the pole, known as *kai sun koon,* or six-and-a-half-point pole. This form maintains within its movements all the essentials of pole fighting: stance development, body mechanics, striking power, accuracy, speed, coordination, timing, distancing, and proper mind-set. The form is meant to be practiced in its entirety, although it is broken down here into smaller sets of connected movements as a learning tool. Thus, it has been divided into the opening salutation and ready position, the main body of the pole form, and the closing sequence.

In order to fully understand and perform this basic pole form, you must have already developed strong basic stances and hand movements. In addition, it is important to hold and maneuver the pole properly before embarking on learning the form.

HOLDING AND MANEUVERING THE POLE

The first thing the Chuka Shaolin exponent is taught in terms of pole use is the proper methods of holding the pole, thrusting the pole, and maneuvering the pole.

Proper Grip

The proper method of holding the pole is in the standard way one would shake hands or hold an everyday hammer. The difference lies in that the pole is held with both hands. The right hand holds the pole anywhere between its center and end depending on use (fig. 1). The left hand holds the pole at its base, with no wood showing past the little finger of the gripping hand (fig. 2).

Fig. 1

Center Thrust

When thrusting the pole forward from the center (and perhaps aiming at the sternum of an opponent), the right hand projects the pole forward with great force, while the left hand retracts slightly. At the completion of this thrusting movement, the pole will be perpendicular to the practitioner's upper body, with the left hand, right hand, and right elbow falling along this center line (figs. 3 and 4).

Fig. 2

Fig. 3

Fig. 4

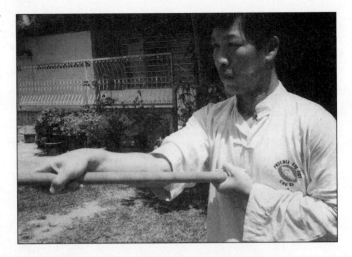

Butt-End Thrust

When using the butt end of the pole for thrusting, the pole must first be brought in line with and parallel to the shoulders in such a way that the right hand is held behind the left hand. Once in this position, the left arm should be fully extended to the front, while the left hand holds the pole so that it can slip through the hand without actually losing contact. The right hand holds the pole, palm up, in much the same way a javelin or spear-thrower chambers his throwing hand prior to launching his spear into the air. The right hand, which is holding fast to the pole, then thrusts forward toward the opponent. The left hand acts as a guide for the pole as it projects toward the target (figs. 5 and 6).

Circling Maneuvers

In an effort to block an opponent's oncoming blows and to deliver blows of one's own, it is often necessary to twirl, circle, and otherwise maneuver the pole around the body and from side to side. However, without the proper technique for doing so, the pole may become trapped in the practitioner's limbs or the practitioner may strike himself with his own weapon. The key to successfully circling the pole around the body is to allow one hand to always fall under the other and then to reverse the action on the other side. The end position in such a striking maneuver finds the exponent's right hand fully extended forward, while the left hand ends up near the armpit and next to the triceps of the right arm (fig. 7).

Fig. 5

Fig. 6

Fig. 7

BREAKDOWN OF THE FORM

For ease of study, the form had been broken down into three sequences of movements: the salutation and ready position, the core movements of the form, and the closing sequence. While each sequence can be studied and learned separately, the form should ultimately be performed in total, with no breaks in timing or rhythm between each sequence.

Part 1: Salutation and Ready Position

Begin the salutation from a standing attention position, hands at your sides, pole on floor to your right (fig. 8). With your hands on your waist, turn to your right (fig. 9) then cross your hands and assume a right hanging-horse stance (fig. 10). Step forward into a left hanging-horse stance and separate your hands (fig. 11). Step back with your left foot until it is parallel to your right foot and bring both hands to the left side of your ribs, with the right hand in a fist (fig. 12). While doing this, step forward into a right hanging-horse stance while extending your hands out in front of your right side (fig. 13). Now, step back with your right leg until it is parallel with your left leg, while pulling your hands back to a chambered position at your right ribs (fig. 14). Complete the salutation by turning 90 degrees to face the forward, assume a left hanging-horse stance, and extend both hands forward to salute again (fig. 15).

Fig. 8

Fig. 9

Fig. 10

Fig. 11

Fig. 12

Fig. 13

Fig. 14

Fig. 15

Next, assume the ready position by lifting your left leg up as you circle your left hand counterclockwise (fig. 16), place your left foot down into a hanging-horse stance and extending your left hand into the ready position.

Fig. 16

Part 2: Core Movements of the Form

Step forward with your right leg to bend down and pick up the koon with both hands (fig. 17). Once the koon is in your hands, pull your right leg back so that you are facing forward in a horse-riding stance holding the koon at waist level and pointing forward (fig. 18).

Step forward with your right leg into a hanging-horse stance as you rotate the koon clockwise, ending with it shoulder height, facing forward (figs. 19–21).

Fig. 17

Fig. 18

Fig. 19

Fig. 20

Fig. 21

Pull the koon back and then thrust it forward by sliding your left hand toward your right as you swing the koon to the left (figs. 22 and 23). Lift your right hand slightly as your left hand thrusts the koon forward (fig. 24). Next, step forward with your right leg and move the koon in a small, counterclockwise and downward circle (right palm down) (fig. 25).

Fig. 22

Fig. 23

Fig. 24

Fig. 25

Pull the koon back clockwise and strike low (to the ankle) while moving into a right hanging-horse stance (fig.26). Step forward with your right leg and thrust the koon forward by pushing your left hand forward (figs. 27 and 28).

Move your left foot out to the side into horse-riding stance and down by pulling the koon down to your left side (fig. 29).

Fig. 26

Fig. 27

Fig. 28

Fig. 29

From here, move your right leg forward into a hanging-horse stance and block by swinging the koon, point up, to the right (fig. 30), and then blocking in the same manner to the left (fig. 31), and then blocking in the center by lowering the koon, with the point facing forward (fig. 32). This center block is immediately followed with a forward thrust (fig. 33).

Fig. 30

Fig. 31

Fig. 32

Fig. 33

Next, step forward with your left foot into a horse-riding stance while pulling your left hand back and striking down to your left side (fig. 34).

Fig. 34

Move forward with your right foot and then turn 90 degrees to your right into a horse-riding stance (fig. 35) as you block past your right hip by pushing your left hand forward and then pulling your right hand down (fig. 36). From here, step forward with your left leg and strike upward with the pole by pulling back with your left hand to hip level (fig. 37). Then block with the koon to your right (fig. 38), then block to your left (fig. 39), then block to your center (fig. 40), countering with a forward thrust of the koon (fig. 41).

You will now turn to face the rear. To do this, step forward with your left leg as you swing the koon clockwise to the right (fig. 42). When the koon reaches about head level, turn 180 degrees to the right (so you are now facing the back) and strike down (fig. 43). Immediately upon downward impact, thrust the koon forward by pushing your left hand forward toward your right hand (fig. 44). From the thrust, you will execute four blocks: first down to your left (fig. 45), then up and to your right (fig. 46), then up and to your left (fig. 47), and then down to your center (fig. 48). This series of blocks is immediately followed by a center thrust of the koon (fig. 49).

Fig. 35

Fig. 36

Fig. 37

Fig. 38

Fig. 39

Fig. 40

Fig. 41

Fig. 42

Fig. 43

Fig. 44

Fig. 45

Fig. 46

Fig. 47

Fig. 48

Fig. 49

Next, slide your right hand up the koon and to your right as your left hand pulls the koon down to the left side of your waist (fig. 50). From this chamber position, thrust left with the other end of koon by pushing with right hand (fig. 51).

From here, move your left foot forward into a hanging-horse stance while turning your body to the right as you swing the koon in a circle behind and over your head to strike down (figs. 52, 53, and 54). This is immediately followed by a center thrust with the koon (fig. 55).

Follow the thrust by pulling the koon back and parallel to the ground with your left hand (fig. 56). Then turn 90 degrees to the right so that you once again face the front (fig. 57). Without hesitation, thrust the koon forward (fig. 58) and then retract it by pulling both arms directly backward (fig. 59).

Fig. 50

Fig. 51

Fig. 52

Fig. 53

Fig. 54

Fig. 55

Fig. 56

Fig. 57

Fig. 58

Fig. 59

Part 3: Closing Sequence

Complete the form by once again performing a salutation. To do this, move your right leg back behind your left leg, assuming a hanging-horse stance, while swinging the koon in a forward circle (figs. 60–63). Twist to the front and step down with your left foot to move into a right hanging-horse stance to simulate a salutation with the weapon in your right hand—your left hand should be held palm open (fig. 64).

Fig. 60

Finish by stepping back with your right leg, holding the koon vertically along your right side, with your left hand raised to face level and held open (fig. 65). Place your left hand by your side (fig. 66).

Fig. 61

Fig. 62

Fig. 63

Fig. 64

Fig. 65

Fig. 66

CHAPTER EIGHT

Application of
Chuka Weapons

The following photographs illustrate the basic applications of standard
Chuka Shaolin weapon combinations. Not every weapon can be used
effectively against every other weapon, although a trained expert can certainly make use of any object and turn it into an effective weapon. Below,
then, are but a few examples of the weapon-on-weapon defensive combinations found within the Chuka Shaolin repertoire.

POLE VS. POLE: TECHNIQUE 1

Square off with your opponent in a right lead hanging-horse stance. Your
pole is held at the bottom with left palm down and in the middle with
right palm up; the tip of the pole is pointing up on a 45-degree angle in
front of your body. Your opponent is standing in a left lead hanging-horse

stance. His pole is held at the bottom with his right palm down and in the middle with left palm up; the tip of his pole is also on a 45-degree angle to his left and slightly back (fig. 1).

Fig. 1

Your opponent strikes at you diagonally forward with his pole by bringing his right hand behind his right hip and swinging his left hand forward toward you. As he does this, you shift into a horse-riding stance by sliding your right leg back, and block the oncoming pole with the section of your pole between your hands by pushing your left hand forward and raising it up, making the pole vertical (fig. 2).

Immediately upon impact, close the distance by stepping toward your opponent with your left leg into a horse-riding stance while at the same time swinging the pole around your head in an effort to strike your opponent in the neck or face with the tip of your pole (fig. 3).

Upon impact with the opponent's head, continue to swing the pole through the target until its full range of motion is completed. At this time, the tip will be pointing behind you and the butt end will be facing your opponent. From here, prepare for a final thrust by pulling back your left leg slightly (fig. 4).

Fig. 2

Fig. 3

Fig. 4

Finish off your opponent by stepping back down with your left leg into a horse-riding stance while thrusting your right hand forward, striking your opponent in the sternum with the butt end of the pole (fig. 5).

Fig. 5

POLE VS. POLE: TECHNIQUE 2

Square off with your opponent in a right lead hanging-horse stance. Your pole is held at the bottom with left palm down and in the middle with right palm up; the tip of the pole is pointing up on a 45-degree angle in front of your body. Your opponent is standing in a right lead hanging-horse stance, facing slightly to the side. His pole is held at the bottom with his left palm down and in the middle with right palm up; the tip of his pole is on a 45-degree angle to his right and held behind him, the butt end is at waist height (fig. 6).

As your opponent steps forward with his right leg and swings his pole at your head, you adjust your stance for stability by stepping back slightly with your right leg and bringing your pole in front of your body, blocking the opponent's pole between your hands (fig. 7).

Fig. 6

Fig. 7

Fig. 8

Immediately upon impact, step forward with your right leg and drop the tip of your pole down onto the crown of your opponent's head (fig. 8).

POLE VS. POLE: TECHNIQUE 3

Square off with your opponent in a left lead horse-riding stance. Your pole is held at the bottom with left palm down and in the middle with right palm up; the tip of the pole is in front of your body and perpendicular to your opponent. Your opponent is standing in a left lead horse-riding stance. His pole is held at the bottom with his left palm down and in the middle with his right palm down; the tip of the pole is on a 45-degree angle facing you (fig. 9).

As your opponent thrusts his pole toward you, you pivot your body and strike down with the tip of your pole onto your opponent's lead hand (fig. 10). Immediately upon impacting your opponent's hand, step forward with your right leg and thrust the tip of your pole into your opponent's throat (fig. 11).

Fig. 9

Fig. 10

Fig. 11

Iron Rulers vs. Long Spear

Square off with your opponent in a right lead hanging-horse stance. Your iron rulers are held in front of your body, your right hand extended in front of your left hand. Your opponent is also standing in a right lead hanging-horse stance. His spear is held at the bottom with his left palm down and in the middle with his right palm down; the tip of his spear is on a 45-degree angle facing you (fig. 12).

Fig. 12

As your opponent steps forward with his right leg and thrusts his spear toward your head, you step forward with your right leg into a horse-riding stance and block his spear by crossing your iron rulers under it, in effect redirecting his spear by pushing along its wooden shaft (fig. 13).

Fig. 13

Immediately upon contact with your opponent's spear, thrust the iron ruler in your right hand into your opponent's stomach, maintain a check on the spear with the iron ruler held in your left hand (fig. 14).

Fig. 14

Twin Knives vs. Long Spear

Square off with your opponent in a right lead hanging-horse stance. Your twin knives are held in front of your body, your right hand extended in front of your left hand. Your opponent is standing in a left lead horse-riding stance. His spear is held at the bottom with his left palm down and in the middle with his right palm down. The tip of his pole is on a 45-degree angle facing you (fig. 15).

Fig. 15

As your opponent steps forward with his right leg and thrusts his spear at your head, quickly close the distance between you by stepping forward with your right leg into a horse-riding stance and block the spear with the knife in your left hand (fig. 16). In the same motion as your left-hand block, swing the knife in your right hand down diagonally, slashing your opponent's neck (fig. 17).

Fig. 16

Fig. 17

FARMER'S HOE VS. LONG SPEAR

Square off with your opponent in a right lead hanging-horse stance. Imagine your hoe is divided into thirds. Hold it with your left palm down at the bottom third and your right palm up at the middle third. The tip of the hoe is held on a 45-degree angle facing your opponent; the cutting edge of the hoe is facing to your left. Your opponent is in a natural stance with his right leg forward. His spear is held at the bottom with his left palm down and in the middle with his right palm up; the tip of the spear is facing you (fig. 18).

Fig. 18

As your opponent steps forward with his right leg into a horse-riding stance and thrusts his spear at your head, you step forward with your right leg into a horse-riding stance while at the same time raising your hoe up to block and deflect the oncoming spear with the section of the hoe's wooden shaft between your hands (fig. 19).

Fig. 19

Immediately upon impact with your opponent's weapon, shuffle forward with your right leg in an effort to further close the distance, while chopping down with your hoe onto the crown of your opponent's head (fig. 20).

Fig. 20

CHAPTER NINE

On Chi Kung Practice

Chi kung refers to general and specific health exercises that combine Buddhist and Taoist elements. Such exercises are viewed as techniques for regulating the body, the mind, and the breath, and involve movement exercises and self-massage to effect changes in one's health. More specifically, chi kung is the art of exercising the *jing* (essence), *chi* (vital energy), and *shen* (spirit). The nucleus of chi kung is the exercise of consciousness and vital energy. Specifically, chi kung exercises combine the practice of *xing* (shape-postures), *yi* (intention or concentration), and *chi* (vital energy). To perform the so-called genuine chi is to exercise the three treasures of the human body (jing, chi, and shen) so as to relieve pain, strengthen the body's constitution, improve intelligence, and prolong life.

Indeed, for centuries in China, people have engaged in the practice of tai chi and chi kung for health, well-being, and the martial arts. To this day, these slow movement exercises and breathing disciplines, used to harness intrinsic energy known as chi, are practiced daily by millions of people in the parks of China and Taiwan. For the martial artist, however, the development of chi is sought for reasons other than health maintenance.

Martial artists look to develop chi as a means of becoming invulnerable to strikes, to make them stronger, and ultimately to enable them to harm an opponent if necessary. To harness and develop their internal power, martial artists practice various chi kung exercises.

Types of Chi Kung

The varieties of chi kung can be divided into four categories each containing three areas. As for a global categorization, there are Buddhist, Taoist, and Confucian chi kung practices.

Within these categories, there are three primary applications of chi kung. In times past, chi kung was used in conjunction with various Chinese martial arts. Practitioners would spend countless hours memorizing the so-called deadly points along the meridian system, and the specific time of day and month of the year during which each point was most effective. This was the prelude to using the secret "death touch" techniques, known as *dim mak,* to maim or kill an opponent.

The primary use of chi kung today is to improve one's health, thus extending life. This is known as medical or healing chi kung, of which there are three subdivisions: (1) external therapy whereby a Chinese doctor would project his own chi into a patient's body to effect a cure; (2) self-training therapy whereby a person would choose a chi kung program and perform the exercises over a period of time to improve his own health; and (3) a combination of external chi kung treatments from a doctor and an individual's chi kung training program. Within the self-practice method, exercises are done in any combination of three ways: slow movements, meditation, and breathing exercises.

The third category is the use of chi kung for various demonstrative purposes. Many chi kung and martial arts masters today use this method for attracting new patients and/or students.

To develop his internal strength and power, the practitioner of Chuka Shaolin engages in the daily practice of chi kung by focusing his mind and intention on his *tan tien* (a place three centimeters below the navel) while assuming the chi kung postures described below.

Regarding Chuka Shaolin, chi kung training exercises are not done during class. However, this does not diminish the importance of such training. In fact, regardless of what is practiced in class, students are urged to practice chi kung every morning before beginning the day's activities. It takes three years of diligent and continuous training to properly develop the chi. The end result: amplified power in strikes and better health and vitality.

Chi Kung Exercises of Chuka Shaolin

The chi kung exercises of Chuka Shaolin are taught to each student on an individual basis. Students of Chuka Shaolin begin their chi kung training after they have been practicing the art for about two or three years. They are taught how to use their tan tien, breathing methods, and how to bring their strength into their fingertips and then down to their feet.

The fundamental chi kung exercise practiced by exponents of Chuka Shaolin is described below. While it is best to breathe naturally through the nose, bringing the air (or chi) down into the tan tien, no specific expansion or contraction method of the lungs or stomach is used. Indeed, maintaining an even and "normal" breathing pattern will garner the best results, making sure one does not hold the breath at any time. It is also vital that you keep a calm and undistracted mind during these exercises. In an effort to release the many thoughts that tend to arise during such practice, it is best to concentrate and focus *all* of your attention on the tan tien area, thus reducing distracting thoughts. While the chi kung exercise requires the forming and holding of various postures, it is important that you do not focus attention on your hands, arms, legs, or any part of the body other than the tan tien. Indeed, the circulation of energy will permeate throughout your body and out through the fingertips naturally.

Fig. 1

There are five positions that will be assumed during the following chi kung exercise. Each position should be held for the length of twenty to thirty breathes, depending on the practitioner's stamina, before twisting to the other side or changing postures.

Begin the chi kung exercise by sitting into a horse-riding stance and facing to your right. Hold your arms in front of your body at a 90-degree angle, palms open and facing up (fig. 1). After a count of twenty to thirty breaths through the nose, turn at the waist to your left—do not change the stance—and breathe through your nose another twenty to thirty times (fig. 2). While remaining in this stance, extend your hands out to your sides, keeping palms up and hands open, and breathe through your nose another twenty to thirty times (fig. 3).

Fig. 2

Fig. 3

Fig. 4

You will now move out of the horse-riding stance and into the hanging-horse stance by sitting onto your right leg and pulling the left leg in. As you assume the hanging-horse stance, turn your torso to the right until your shoulders and hips are aligned. Then, with arms fully extended, point your left hand diagonally down and your right hand diagonally up (fig. 4). After a count of twenty to thirty breaths through the nose, turn to your right and assume a right lead hanging-horse stance, with arms fully extended, your right hand pointing diagonally down and your left hand pointing diagonally up. Take another twenty to thirty breaths through the nose (fig. 5).

Fig. 5

The exercise is completed by standing up, feet shoulder-width apart, and breathing in and out while expanding and contracting the chest. When breathing in (expanding the chest), move onto the balls of your feet and extend your arms out to your sides with wrists bent forward (fig. 6). When breathing out (contracting the chest), drop to the flats of your feet and at the same time lower your arms to your sides (fig. 7).

Fig. 6

Fig. 7

CHAPTER TEN

On Injury Healing

According to the Chinese Taoist philosophy of *yin* and *yang,* the world is composed of opposites: up and down, hot and cold, strong and weak, male and female. Rather than opposites, though, these terms are actually relativistic in nature. After all, there is no up without down; there is no hot without cold; there is no strong without weak; and there is no male without female. A more precise description of the Taoist philosophy of yin and yang, then, is one of complements.

Regarding the fighting arts philosophy throughout China's history and culture, no skill of killing is attained without also attaining at least a fundamental skill in techniques of healing. Indeed, many of China's martial arts masters are also doctors of traditional Chinese medicine. Such traditional healing practices generally include any combination of chi kung exercises, acupuncture, massage, bone-setting, meditation, and herbology.

It is also widely held that truly good kung-fu has more to do with healing and chi than with fighting. It is believed that those who practice kung-fu but do not also practice chi kung will have nothing when they become old. Without continued and prolonged practice of chi kung the body will break down from wear and tear and one will be unable to effectively perform their martial art, or even daily tasks, as a senior citizen. However, if one practices chi kung and also learns the healing tradition of Chuka Shaolin, they will not only be healthy when they are senior in age but will also have the ability to help others.

Philosophically speaking, exponents of Chuka Shaolin believe that if one knows how to harm a person he should also know how to heal him. It is a matter of adhering to the yin and yang philosophy of balance. In Chinese kung-fu, chi and healing are of vital importance. In fact, they are so important that the most senior exponents of Chuka Shaolin today—Cheong Cheng Leong and Tan Hun Poy—are also traditional Chinese doctors. By Chinese beliefs, then, the art of Chuka Shaolin is considered a complete and well-rounded discipline, encompassing both a fighting art and healing art, and Cheong Cheng Leong and Tan Hun Poey are considered fully evolved masters as a result of having mastered both dimensions. While there is no specific name attached to the healing dimension of Chuka Shaolin, it encompasses the aforementioned chi kung exercises, impact slapping, massage, and herbology.

The Chuka Healing Art

Cheong Cheng Leong began learning the healing dimension of Chuka Shaolin from Master Lee Siong Pheow when Cheong was eighteen years old and already quite advanced in kung-fu. Master Lee asked Cheong, and his classmate Tan Hun Poey (fig. 1), to help him with picking special herbs on a designated Penang hillside. After gathering the herbs, Cheong and Tan would cut and dry them for Master Lee. They would then take the herbs to a local Chinese medicine shop in town and have them ground into powders of varying consistencies.

Fig. 1

At first, Master Lee did not allow Cheong and Tan to assist him with the healing of patients. But when the patients would come to see Master Lee for a treatment, Cheong and Tan were inevitably present and would just sit and observe the healing session. After some time, though, Master Lee saw that the two teenagers held a strong interest in the healing art, and he began to explain to them the hows and whys of healing different patients with various ailments. Then, after some time, Lee eventually allowed Cheong Cheng Leong and Tan Hun Poey to work on patients themselves.

Although Cheong Cheng Leong is the grandmaster of Chuka Shaolin, and is a master of both its fighting and healing arts, only for direct students and close friends does he perform healing treatments. In wanting the art to be preserved and promoted in its fullest, Cheong prefers to concentrate on teaching and imparting the physical fighting art. The healing art is headed by Master Tan Hun Poey. Cheong advises those students who care to study the healing art to do so under the direction of Master Tan.

The healing art of Chuka Shaolin is good for treating old injuries, like an old back or shoulder problem. Exponents of Chuka Shaolin believe that merely removing pain from a person's legs and arms with manipulation or massage is elementary healing, anybody can do it. But with an old injury— one that is more than ten years old—a person often suddenly feels excruciating pain. This occurs when an injury was received at a young age and was never properly treated or allowed to heal. As a result, the injury has become "locked" deep within the musculoskeletal system of the body, being somewhat bothersome all along but unexpectedly surfacing in full force a decade or so later. This happens because, as one gets older, chi is not only depleted but blocked in the muscles, which means one feels the pain more than when they were young and physically active.

The Chuka Shaolin healing art is very specific to the types of ailments it can effectively remedy. It is not effective for curing organic diseases or viruses. Rather, it is concerned solely with the healing and repairing of old injuries to the body's musculoskeletal system.

There are two specific healing methods that are used when treating old injuries: slapping and massage. If it is a new injury, massage will do. But if it is an old injury, you have to slap the injured location with the back of the hand to get through the muscle and energy blockage, which is quite deep by this point. Although it depends on the seriousness of the injury, sometimes a patient will need only one treatment; however, three consecutive treatment sessions are best. Chuka healers have found that, where old injuries are concerned, one slapping treatment is more effective than ten deep-tissue massages.

Fig. 2

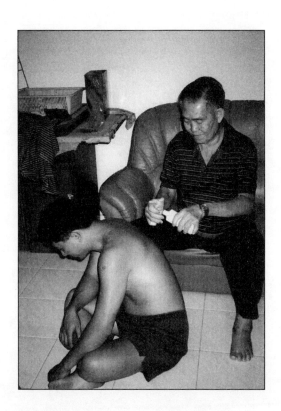

Before and during the impact-slapping procedure, the Chuka healer applies a homemade liniment of wine and herbs on and around the injured area so as to keep the blood flowing, stimulate the chi, and keep the area from bruising again (fig. 2). While slapping the patient's injured area (figs. 3 and 4), if there is truly a bad and old injury, the healer will feel a lot of heat coming out of the area. Once the release of heat is felt, the slapping stops. Since the healer is also skilled in the fighting art of Chuka Shaolin, he cannot strike a patient very hard for fear of causing a secondary injury. Thus, the healer slaps lightly but repeatedly while projecting his chi into the injured area. After hitting, if a lump and veins appear and the healer can see the wound, the chi will then be able to flow freely. The blockage is now open and the body is once again balanced.

Fig. 3

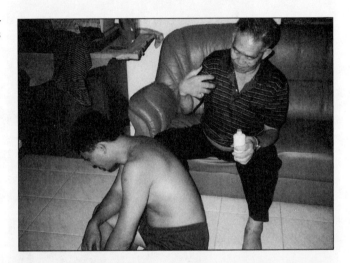

Fig. 4

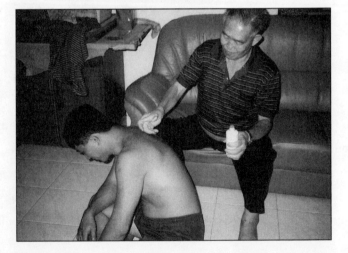

After the slapping is complete and a bump appears on the injured area (fig. 5), liniment is again applied, followed by the application of a home-made herbal paste (fig. 6), which is then covered with a cloth for one night (fig. 7). The paste hardens and can easily be removed the following day, at which point the medicine has had a chance to effectively seep into the body and stimulate the healing process.

Fig. 5

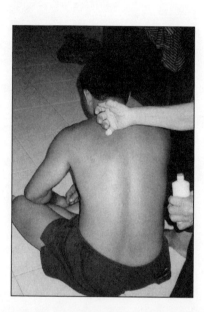

Fig. 6

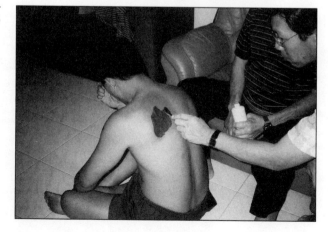

Fig. 7

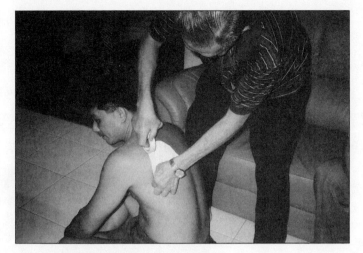

Afterword

The martial arts are ways of life. Indeed, the only way to become proficient and eventually master the martial arts is to immerse yourself in them body, mind, and spirit. There is an old saying in Chinese kung-fu circles, that when you begin the martial arts you are a regular person. After training for a while you become a person with kung-fu. Then, after several more years of training you become a kung-fu person. Only after you have truly consumed and mastered the art do you go full circle and once again become a regular person. At this point, you have become one with the true essence of the martial arts: a free-flowing, spontaneous, and ever-evolving entity.

As a good kung-fu practitioner, one has to be humble socially but aggressive in a fight. In the present society, no matter how good you have trained in the martial arts, you must never go looking for trouble. What, then, is the point of training in these arts and developing these fighting skills? Self-development and evolution through the unremitting discipline that is necessary to mastering the martial arts over a lifetime.

It must be understood, however, that learning martial arts without practicing chi kung training is a waste of time, for when you become old you will have nothing to show for your lifelong practice and devotion. Moreover, it is also advisable to become proficient in a healing modality, so that one may help others. As we have already discussed, possessing the ability to heal others is the balancing factor of knowing how to injure them. Indeed, one who is only versed in the fighting art, and not its collateral chi kung health aspect or healing dimension, can never come to truly understand and master the art or become a fully evolved human being.

We hope, then, that this book has exposed to the reader interested in this rare and dynamic art a broader side of the art and some of the things necessary to master it: fighting principles, basics, two-person fighting form, pole form, weapon applications, chi kung discussion and exercise, and a presentation of the healing art.

For those who possess a sincere interest and desire to learn more about Chuka Shaolin, please feel free to contact the authors care of the publisher.

Lineage of Chuka Shaolin

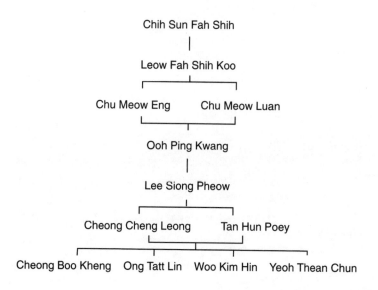

Chih Sun Fah Shih
|
Leow Fah Shih Koo

Chu Meow Eng   Chu Meow Luan

Ooh Ping Kwang
|
Lee Siong Pheow

Cheong Cheng Leong   Tan Hun Poey

Cheong Boo Kheng   Ong Tatt Lin   Woo Kim Hin   Yeoh Thean Chun

The Forms of Chuka Shaolin

SOLO EMPTY-HAND FORMS

kai san chien (opening the mountain)

er shih sze tien (twenty-four points, number one)

er shih sze tien (twenty-four points, number two)

hu chao chien (tiger claw, ascending tiger)

hu chao chien (tiger claw, descending tiger)

loong hu chien (dragon and tiger)

ta choong koong (stamping inside, the palace being surrounded)

mei hua chien (plum blossom)

lien huang tuei (continuous kicks)

tong tze pai kwan yin (boy paying respects to the goddess of mercy)

yin yan er sien ku (two positive and negative heavenly ladies)

ta ooh li (strength performance)

shih pa lohan chien (eighteen hands of the lohan)

foong yen tin sun chien (phoenix-eye fist guarding the mountain)

shih ta hsing hsian (ten animals fighting movements)

TWO-MAN EMPTY-HAND FORMS

kung sow twee chai (prearranged sparring, set one)

kung sow twee chai (prearranged sparring, set two)

SOLO WEAPON FORMS

liu tien pan koon (six-and-a-half-point pole)

mei hua koon (plum blossom pole)

sho ho chian (neck locking long spear)

shih sun chian (thirteen-points long spear)

chu toh (farmer's hoe)

tze mu tau (double knives)

tieh cher (iron rulers)

TWO-MAN WEAPON FORM

koon twee chai (prearranged pole pattern)

Glossary of Chuka Shaolin Terms

The following is a glossary of the Chuka Shaolin terms found within this book. They are presented first in English and then in Mandarin.

double dragon two-finger strike	*swang-loon*
deflect or block	*kher*
double-palm block	*swang kher chang*
double phoenix-eye fist strike	*swang fung yen*
energy-building exercises	*chi kung*
essence	*jing*
farmer's hoe	*chu toh*
field of elixir	*tan tien*
forward horse	*chin-ma*

hand techniques	*sou fa*
hanging-horse stance	*tiow ma*
high and low-wrist block	*yin yan tiow kher shou*
horse-riding stance	*ma pu*
intention	*yi*
iron rulers	*tieh cher*
lightning kick	*san-tien chiau*
long spear	*ch'iang*
low block	*sia kher shou*
middle-palm block	*zhong aun chang*
palm heel	*chang*
phoenix-eye fist kung-fu	*Chuka Shaolin*
phoenix-eye fist strike	*fung yen*
pole	*koon*
ready position	*choon pei*
salutation	*ching*
shape postures	*xing*
single-palm block	*tuoh chang*
six-and-a-half-point pole	*kai sun koon*
solo empty-hand forms	*chuan-tao*
spirit	*shen*
thrust-penetrate-tear hand	*cha ching shou*
twin knives	*tze mu tau*
two-person prearranged sparring	*kung sow twee chai*
upper-palm block	*sun tuoh chang*
upper-wrist block	*sun kher shou*
vital energy	*chi*